APRIL 50 COLORING PAGES FOR OLDER KIDS RELAXATION

SHIH CHIEN HUA

PUBLISHED BY:
SHIH CHIEN HUA
Copyright © 2018

SEABIRD SHOP >50FOR

FB FAN PAGE

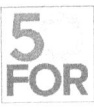

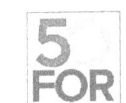

Disclaimer
The information contained in this book is for general information purposes only. The information is provided by the authors and while we endeavor to keep the information up to date and correct, we make no representations or warranties of any kind, express or implied, about the completeness, accuracy, reliability, suitability or availability with respect to the book or the information, products, services, or related graphics contained in the book for any purpose. Any reliance you place on such information is therefore strictly at your own risk.

APRIL 1ST

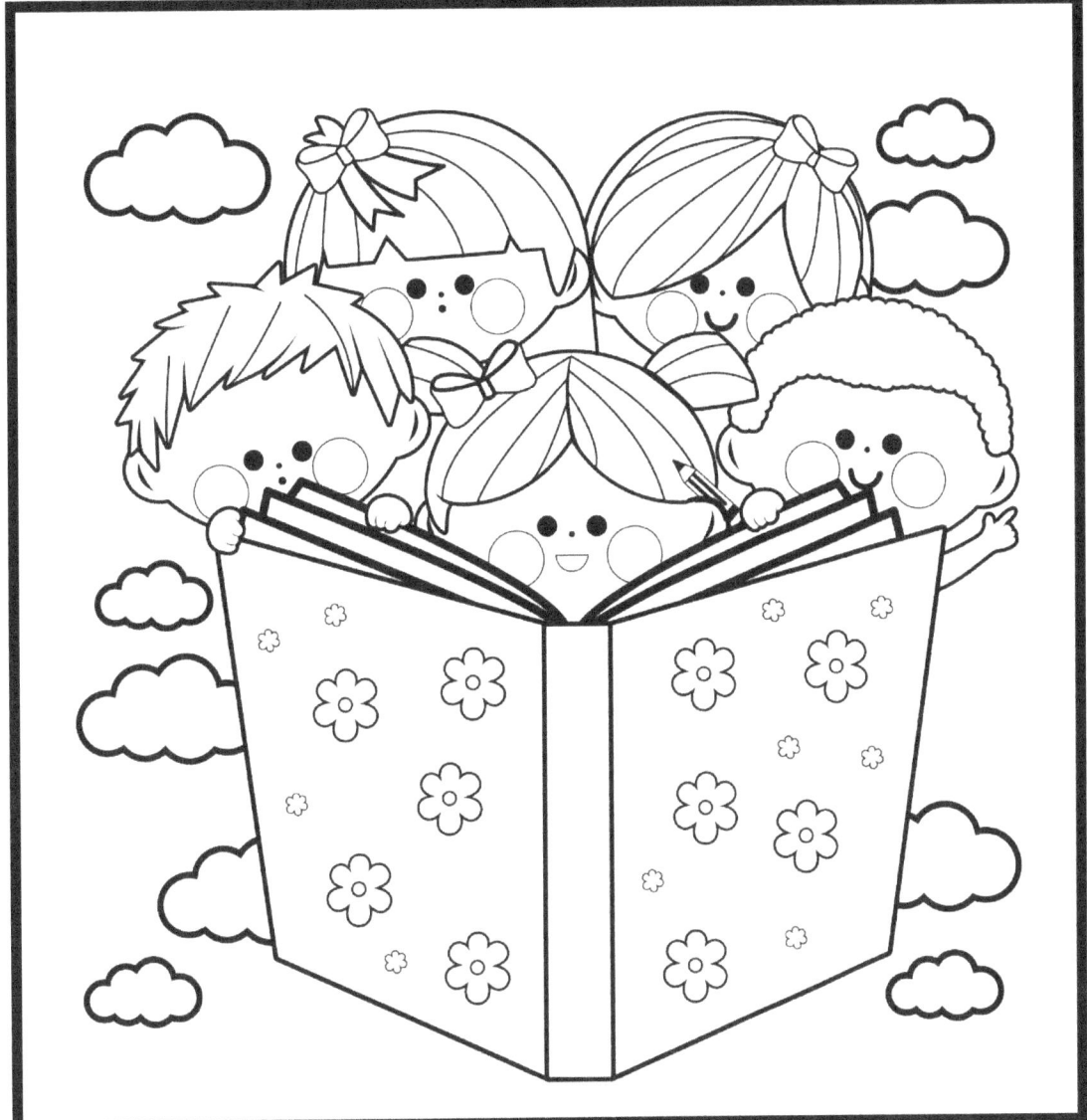

note:

_____

_____

_____

APRIL 2ND

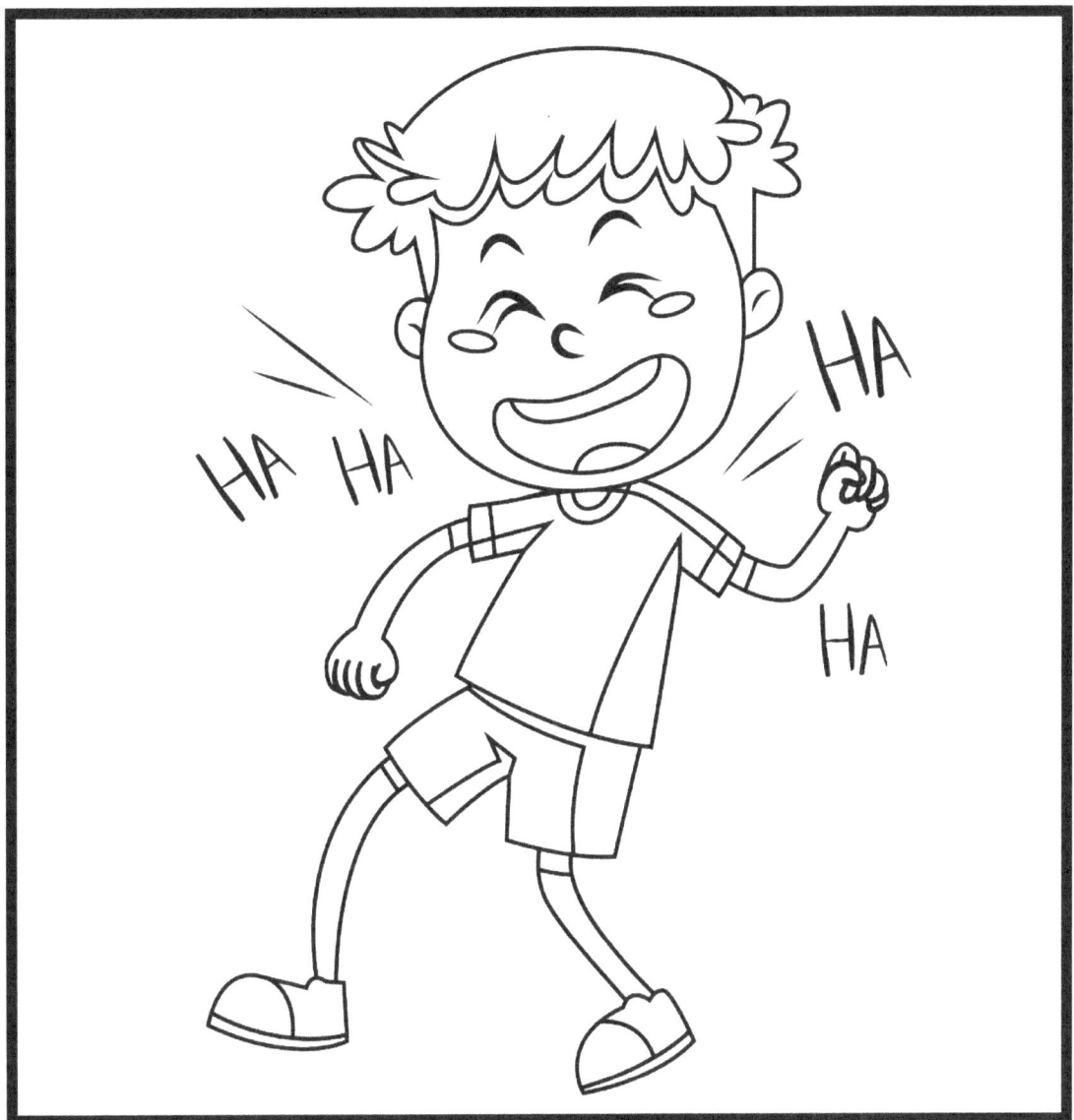

note:

_____

_____

_____

APRIL 3RD

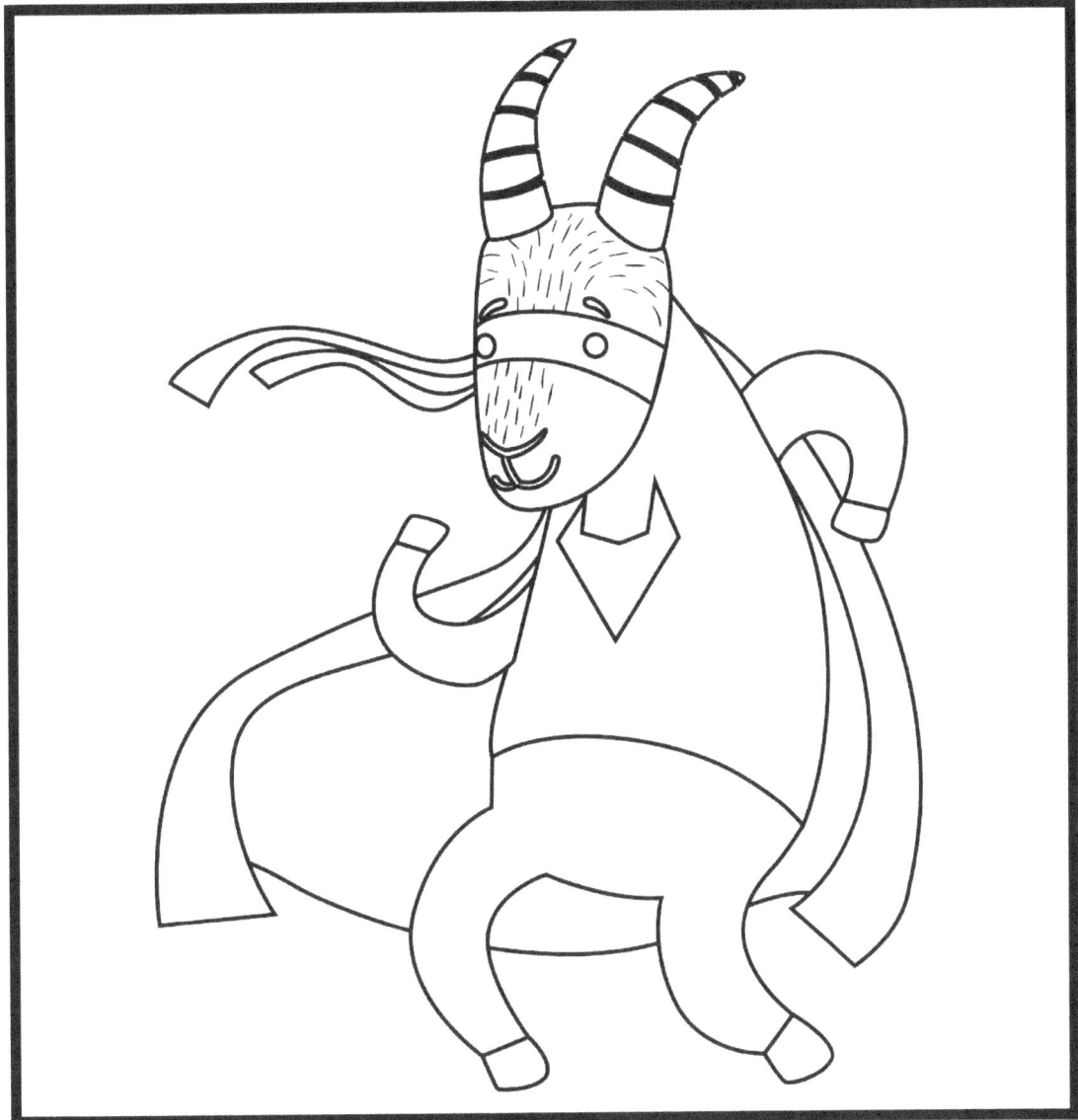

note:

_____

_____

_____

APRIL 4TH

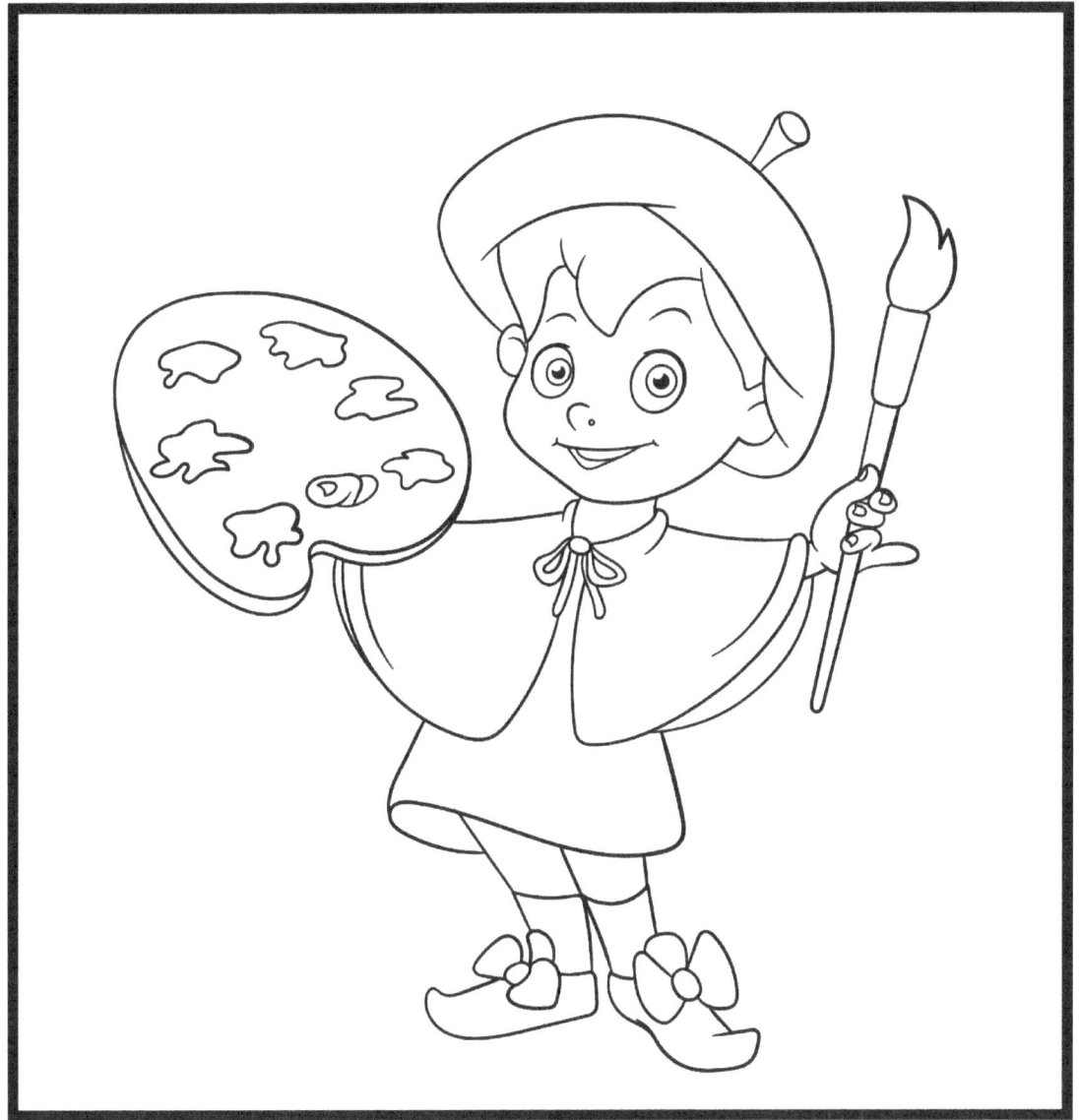

note:

_____

_____

_____

APRIL 5TH

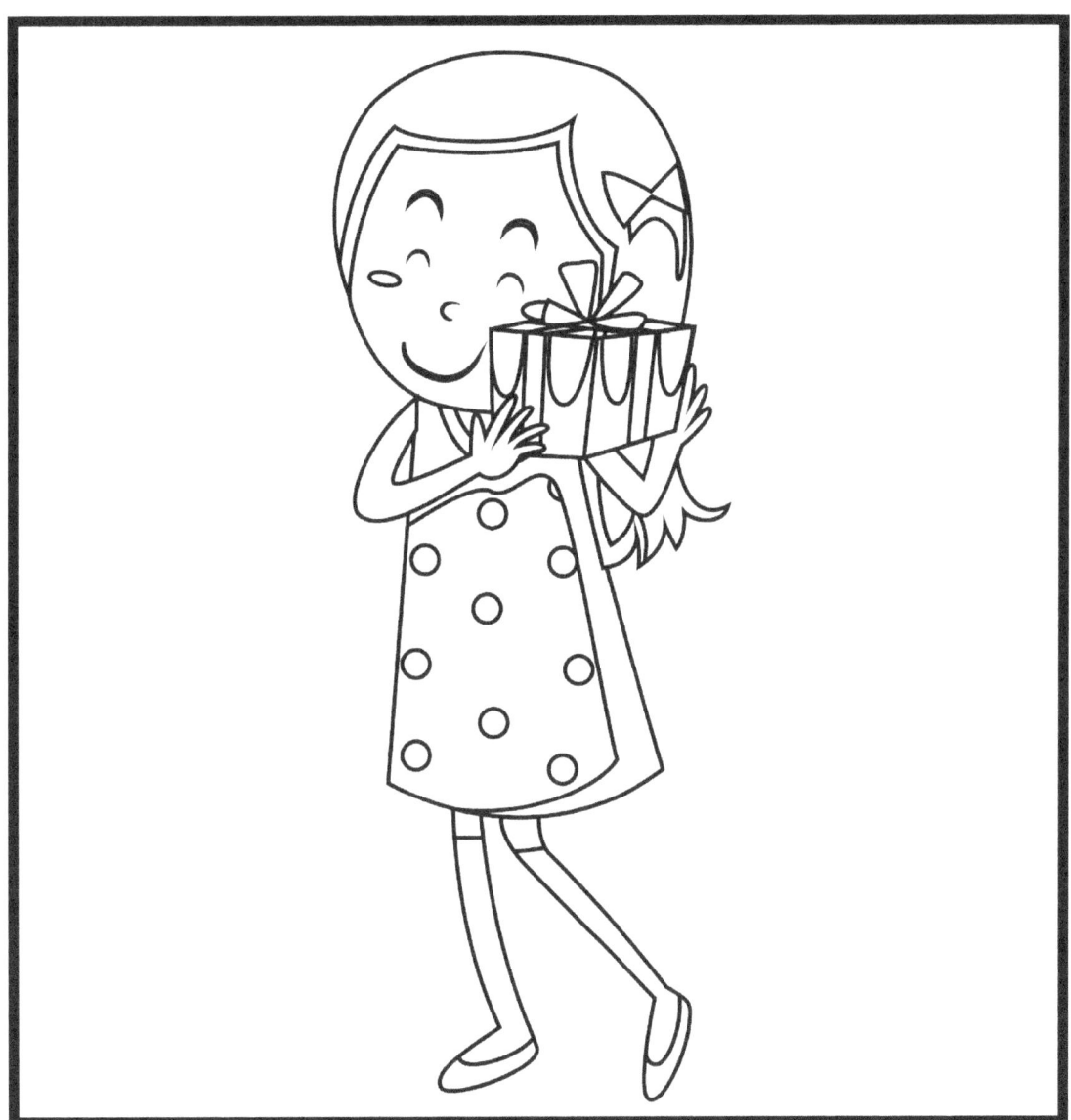

note:

_____

_____

_____

APRIL 6TH

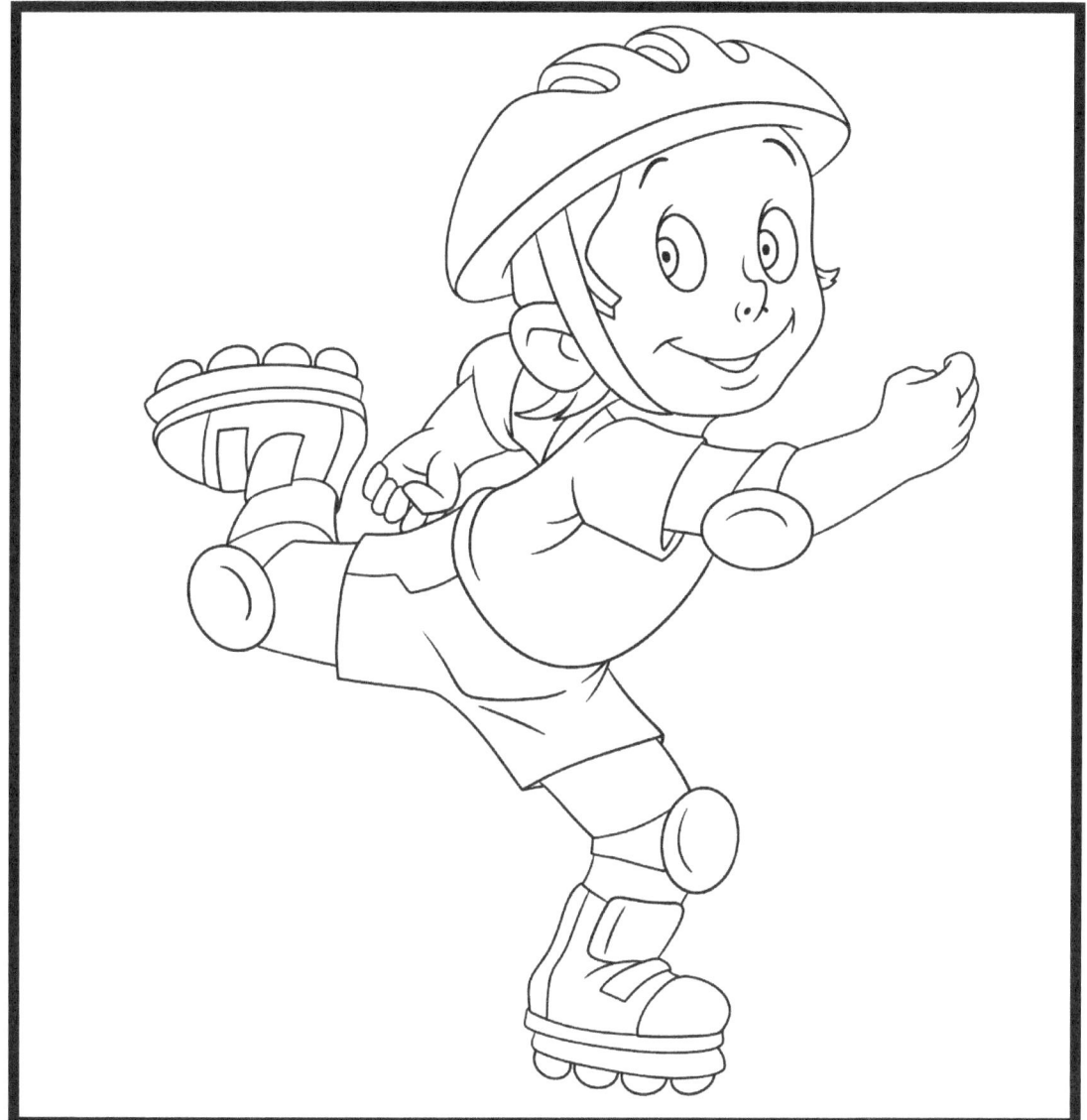

note:

_____

_____

_____

APRIL 7TH

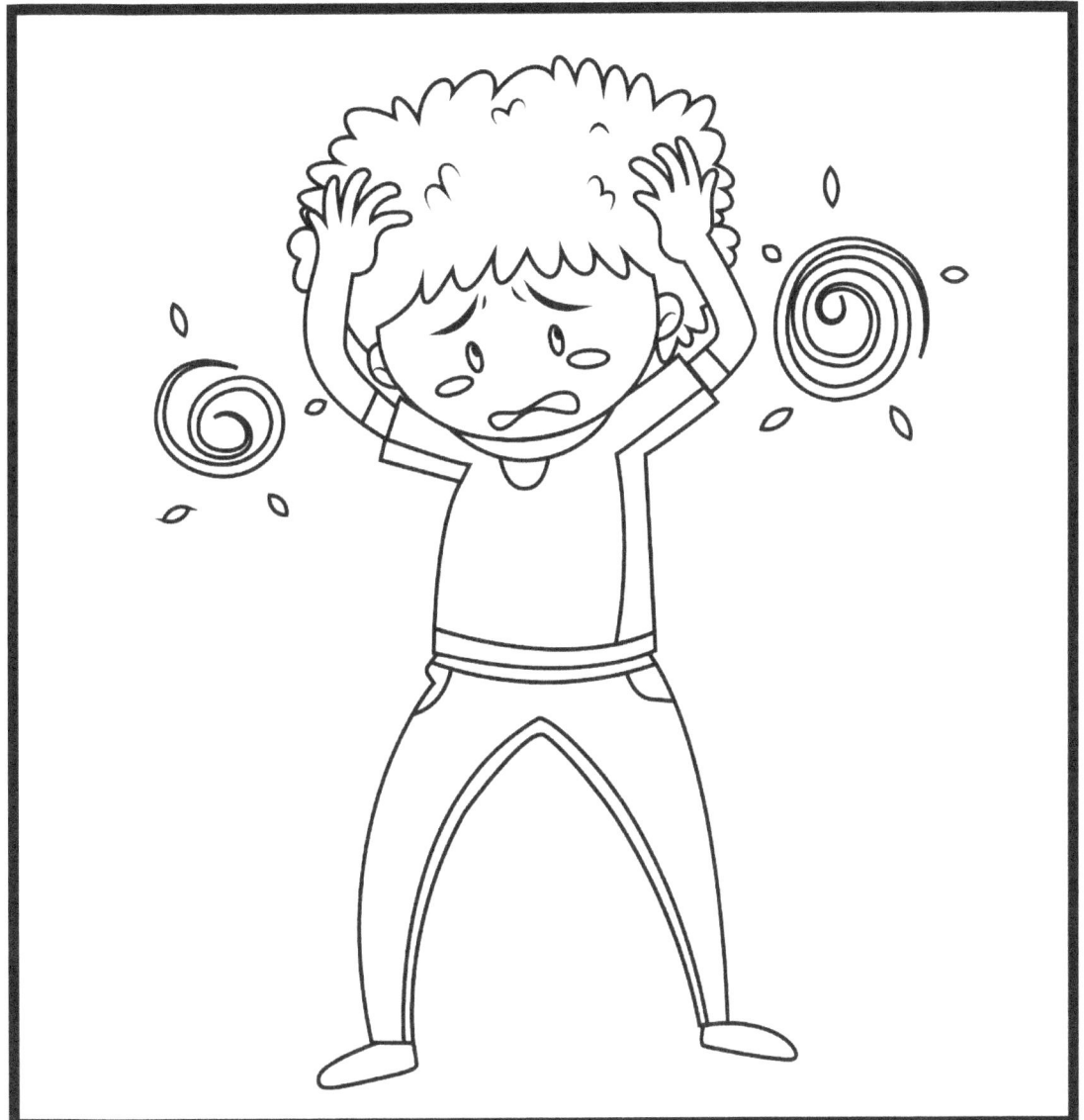

note:

_____

_____

_____

APRIL 8TH

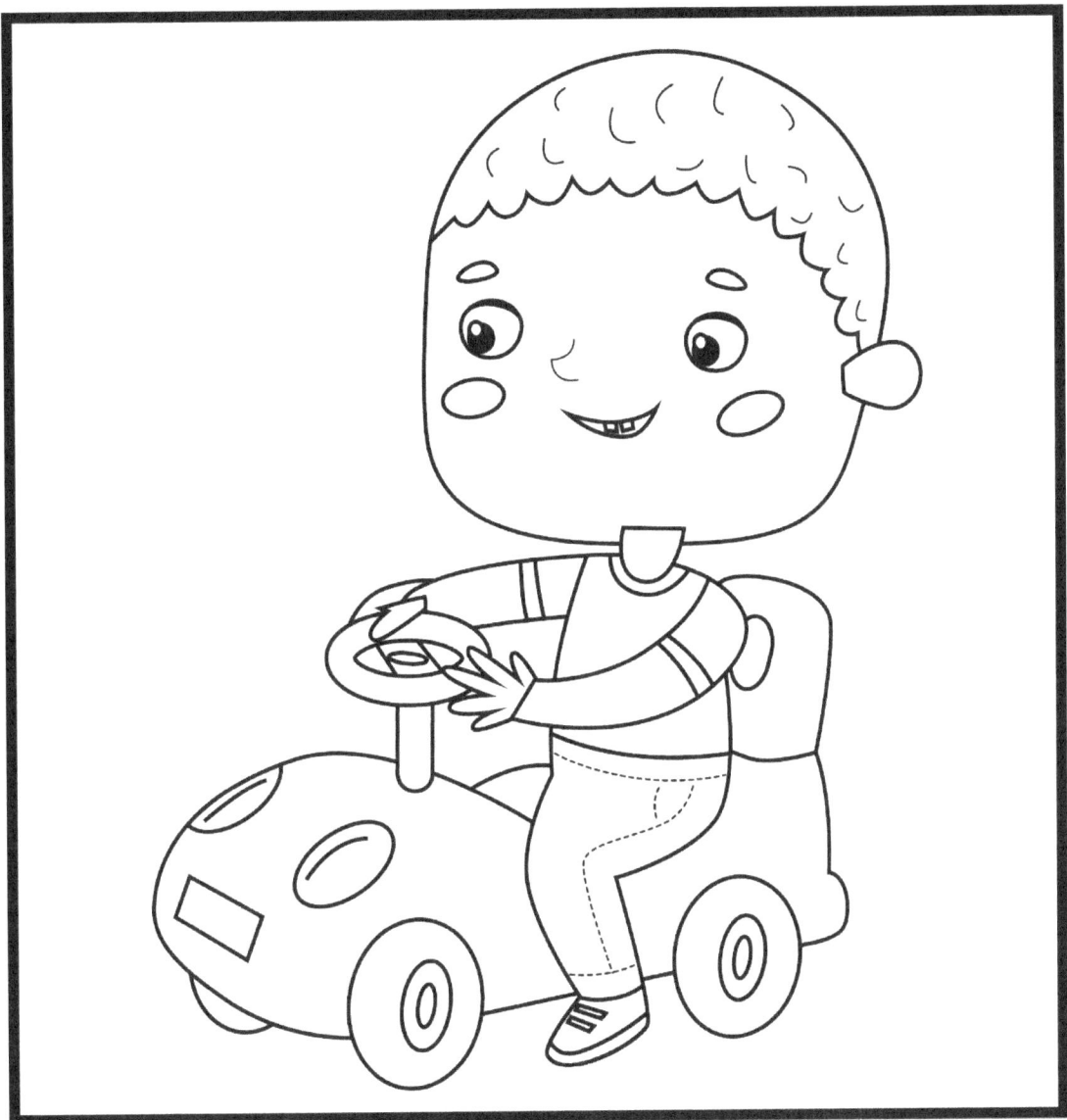

note:

_____

_____

_____

APRIL 9TH

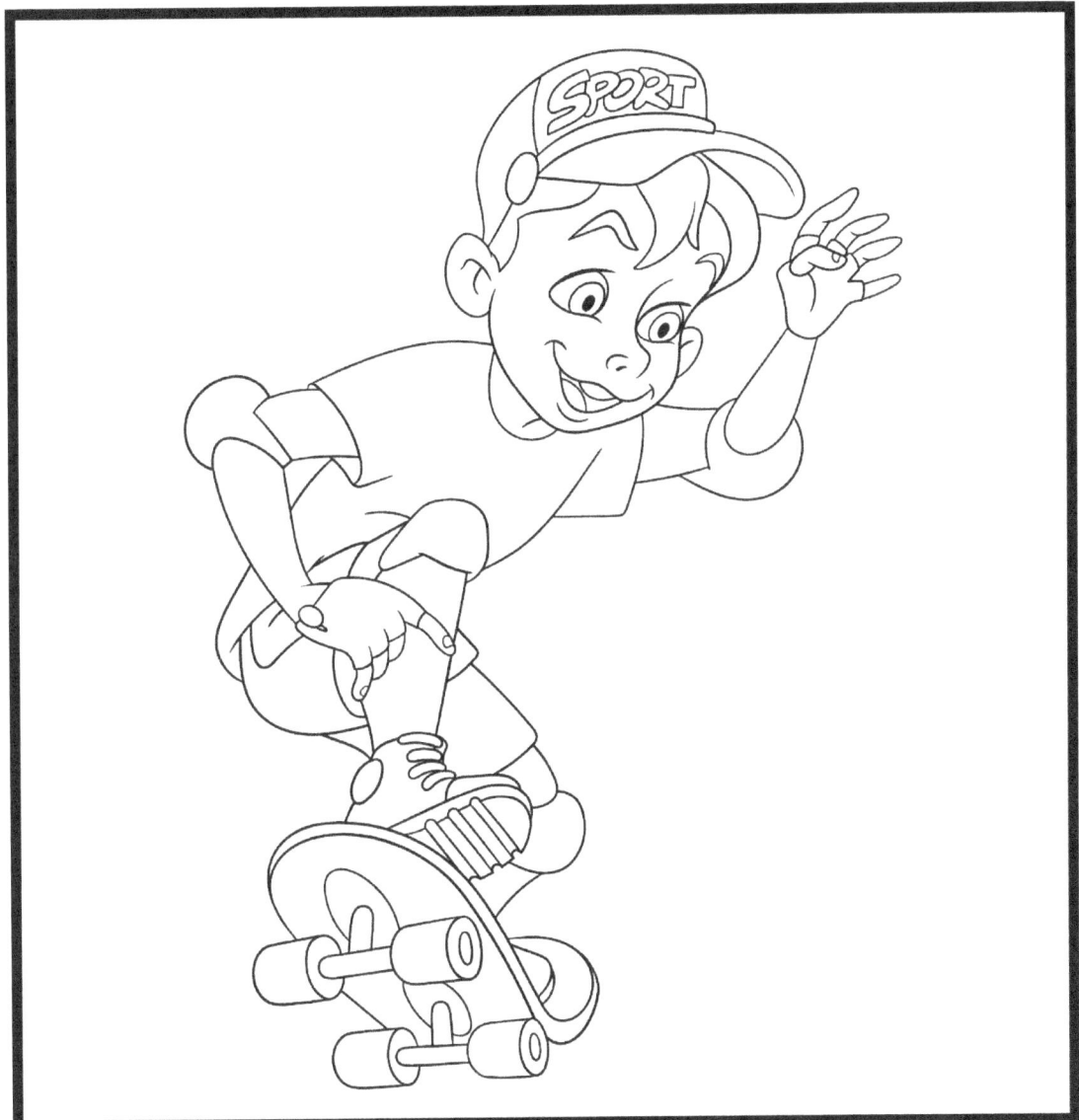

note:

_____

_____

_____

APRIL 10TH

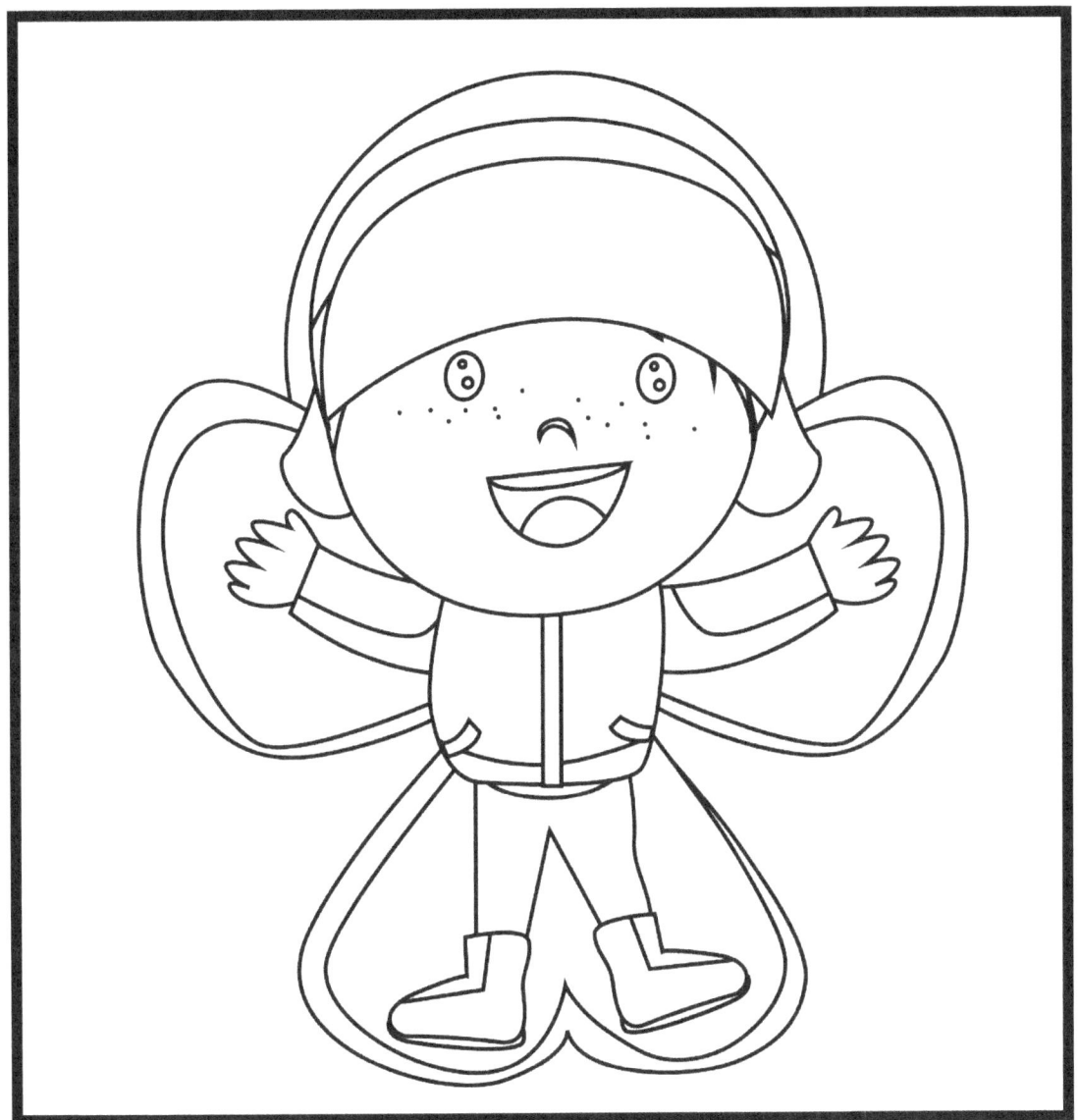

note:

_____

_____

_____

APRIL 11TH

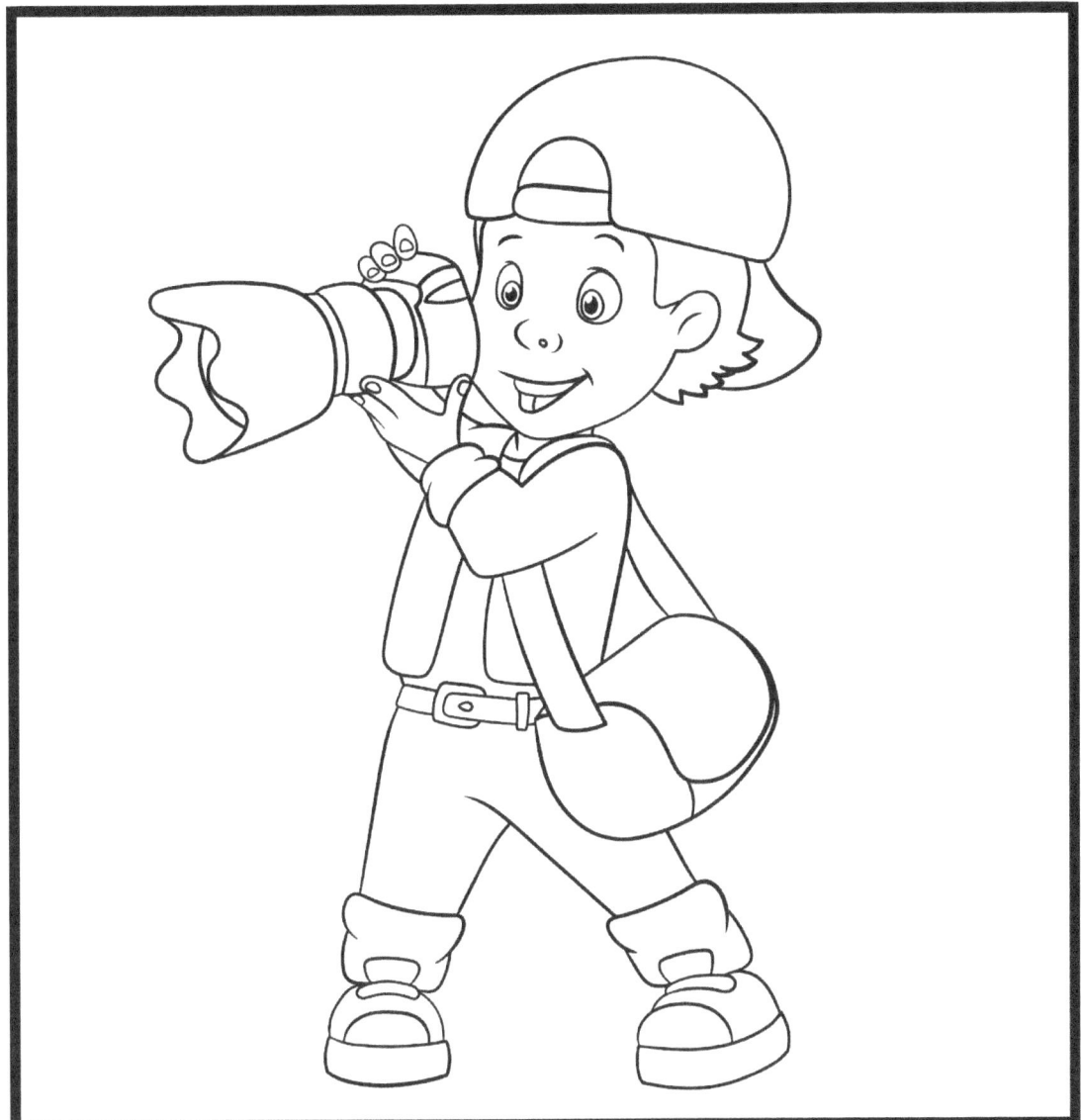

note:

_____

_____

_____

APRIL 12TH

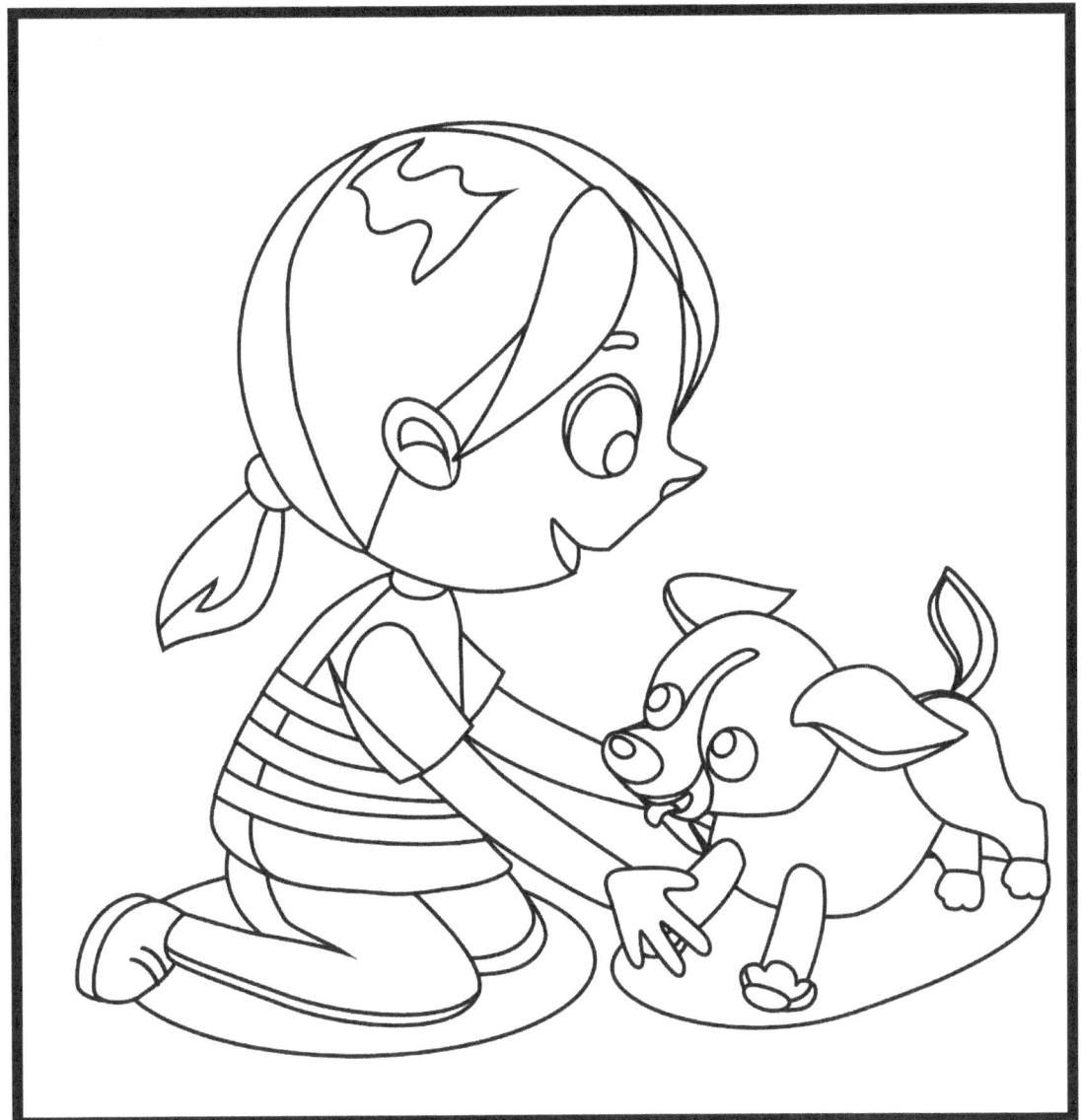

note:

_____

_____

_____

APRIL 13TH

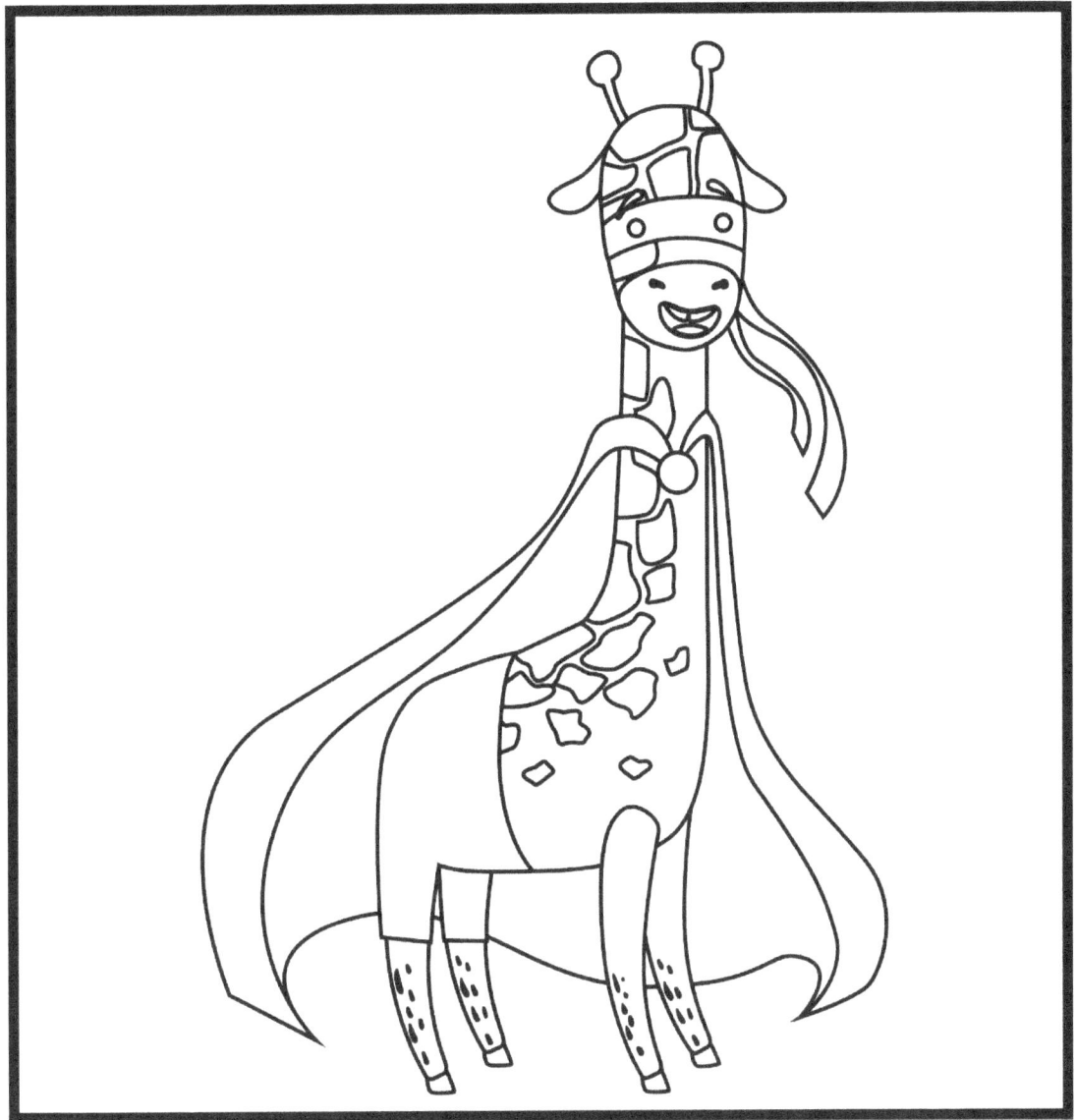

note:

_____

_____

_____

APRIL 14TH

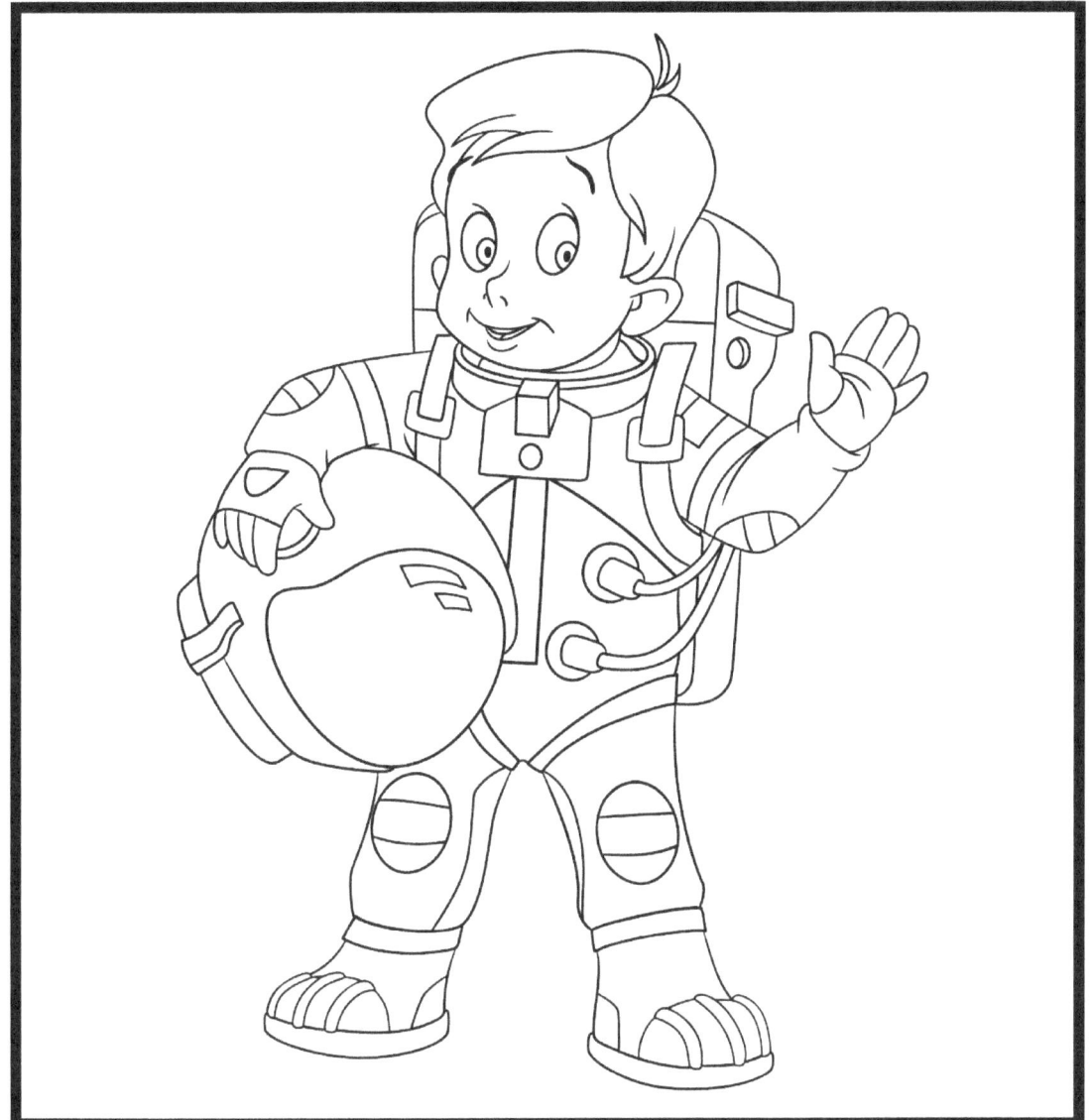

note:

_____

_____

_____

APRIL 15TH

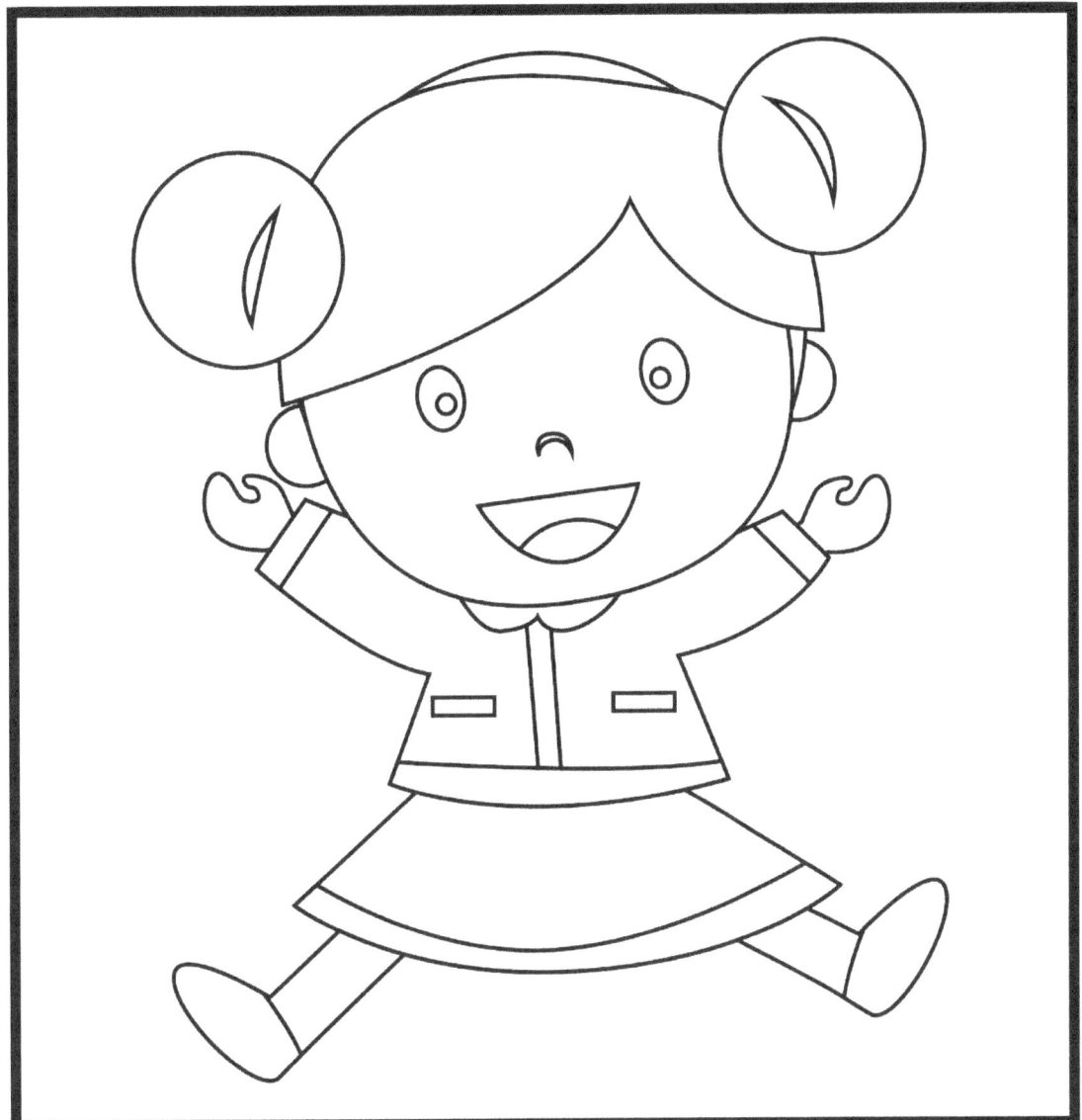

note:

_____

_____

_____

APRIL 16TH

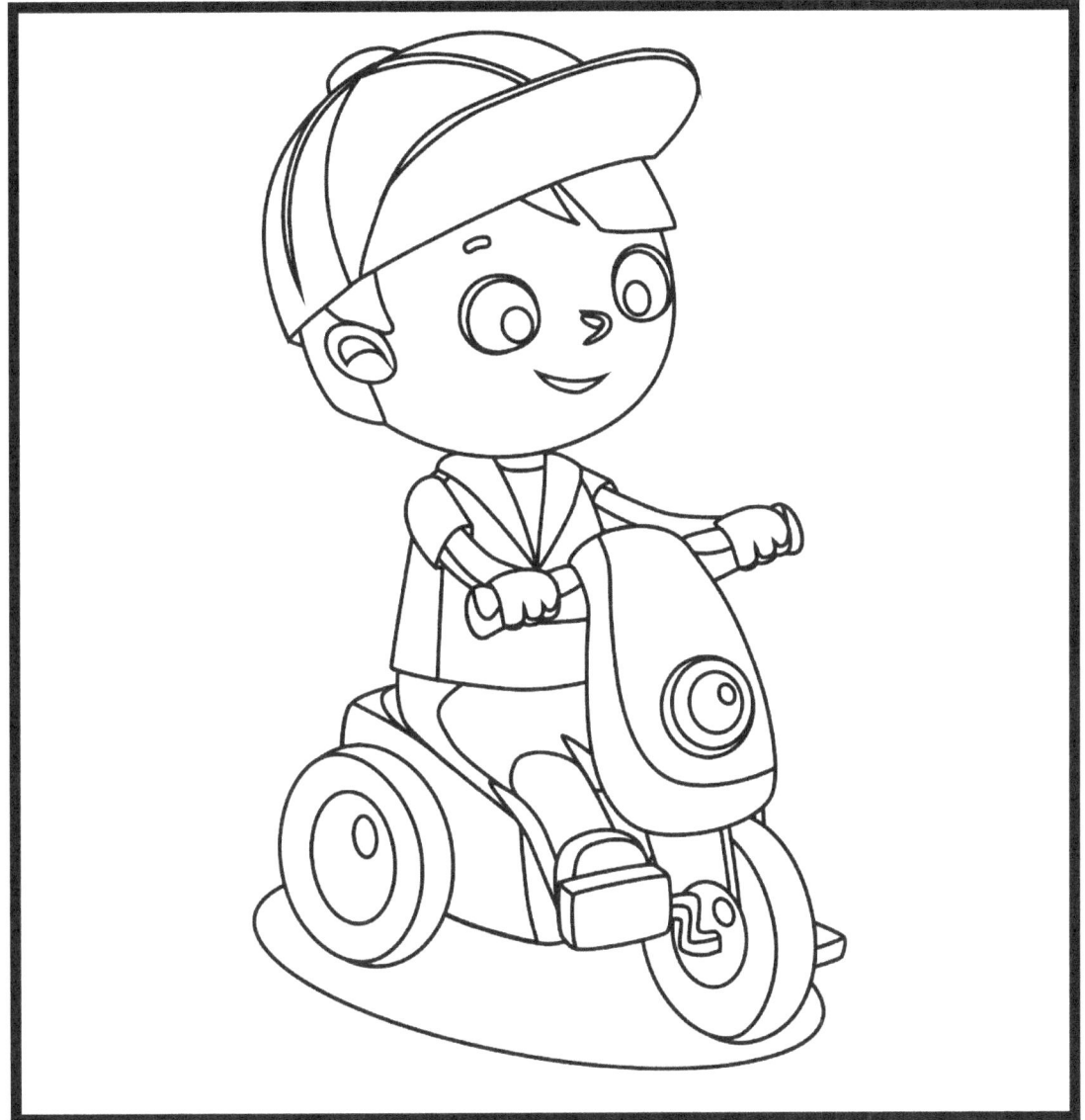

note:

_____

_____

_____

APRIL 17TH

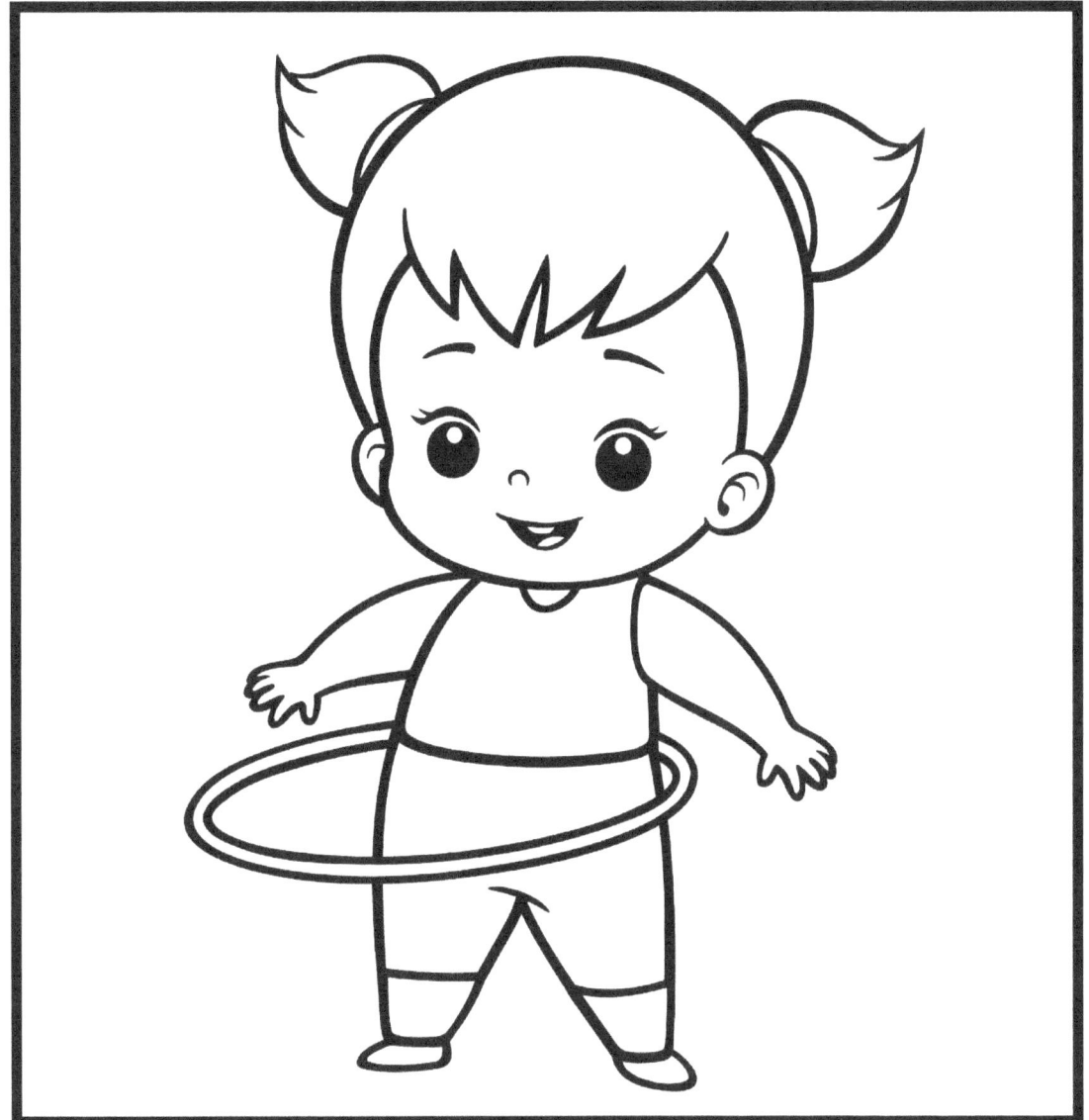

note:

_____

_____

_____

APRIL 18TH

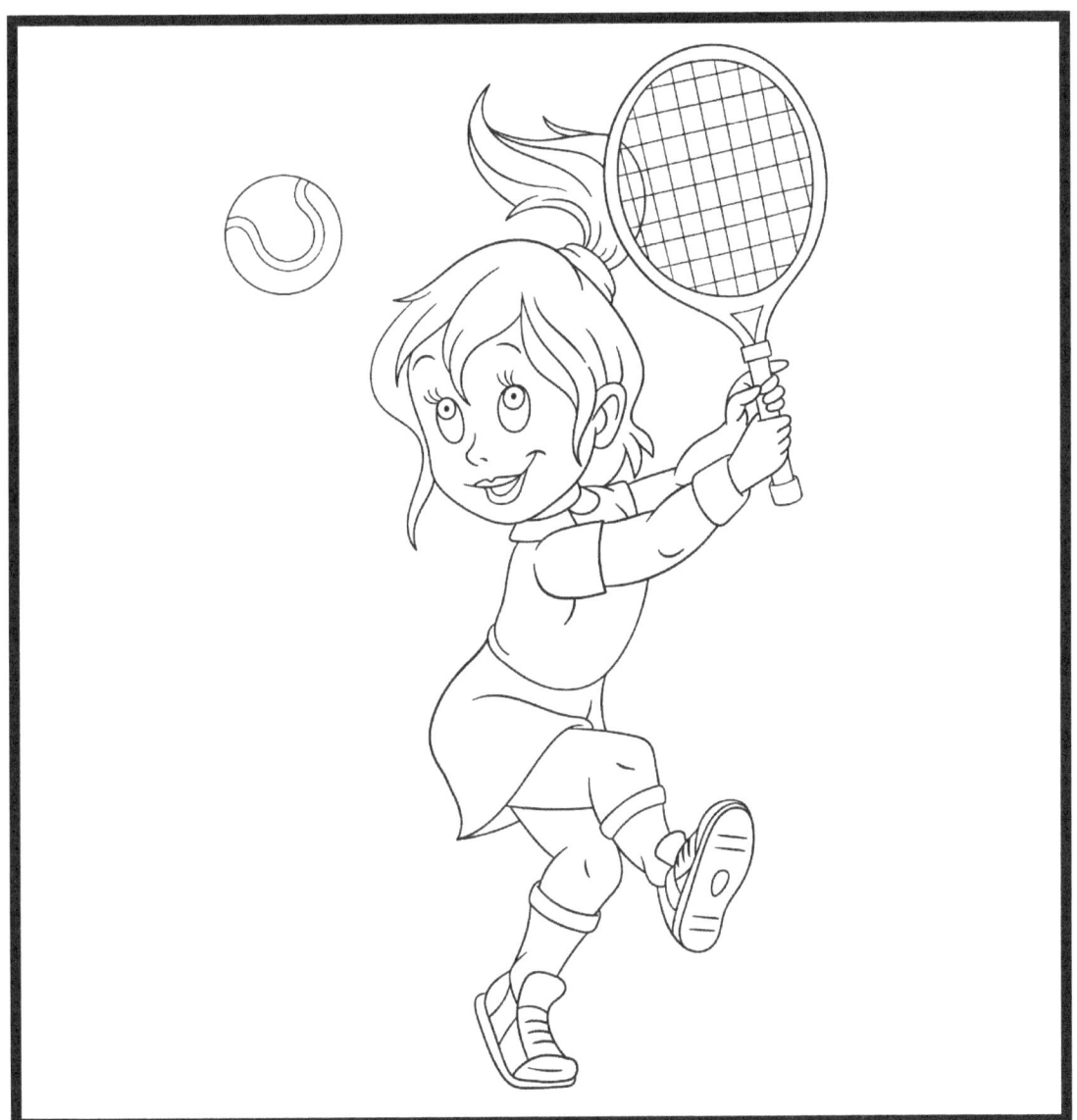

note:

_____

_____

_____

APRIL 19TH

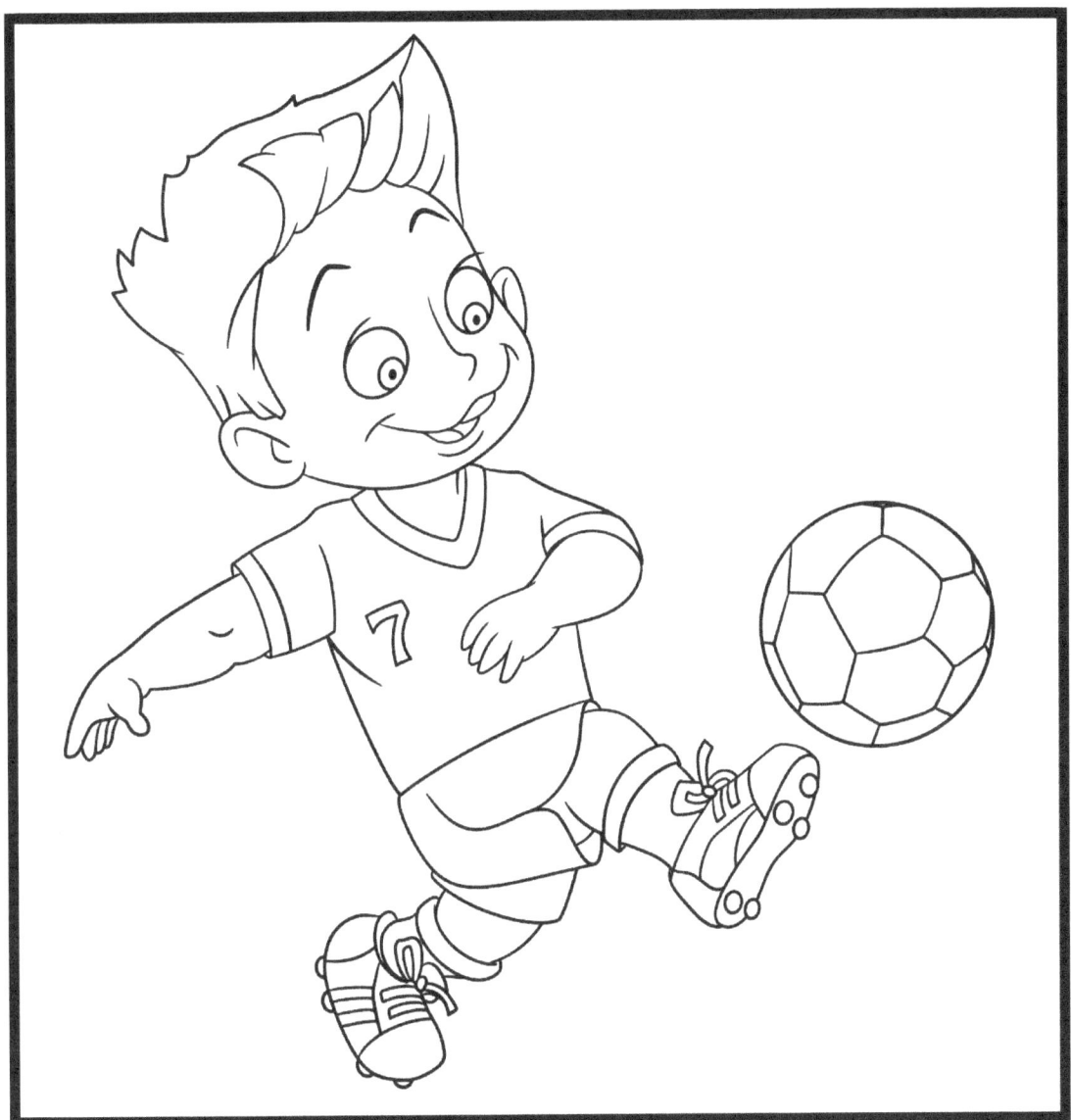

note:

_____

_____

_____

APRIL 20TH

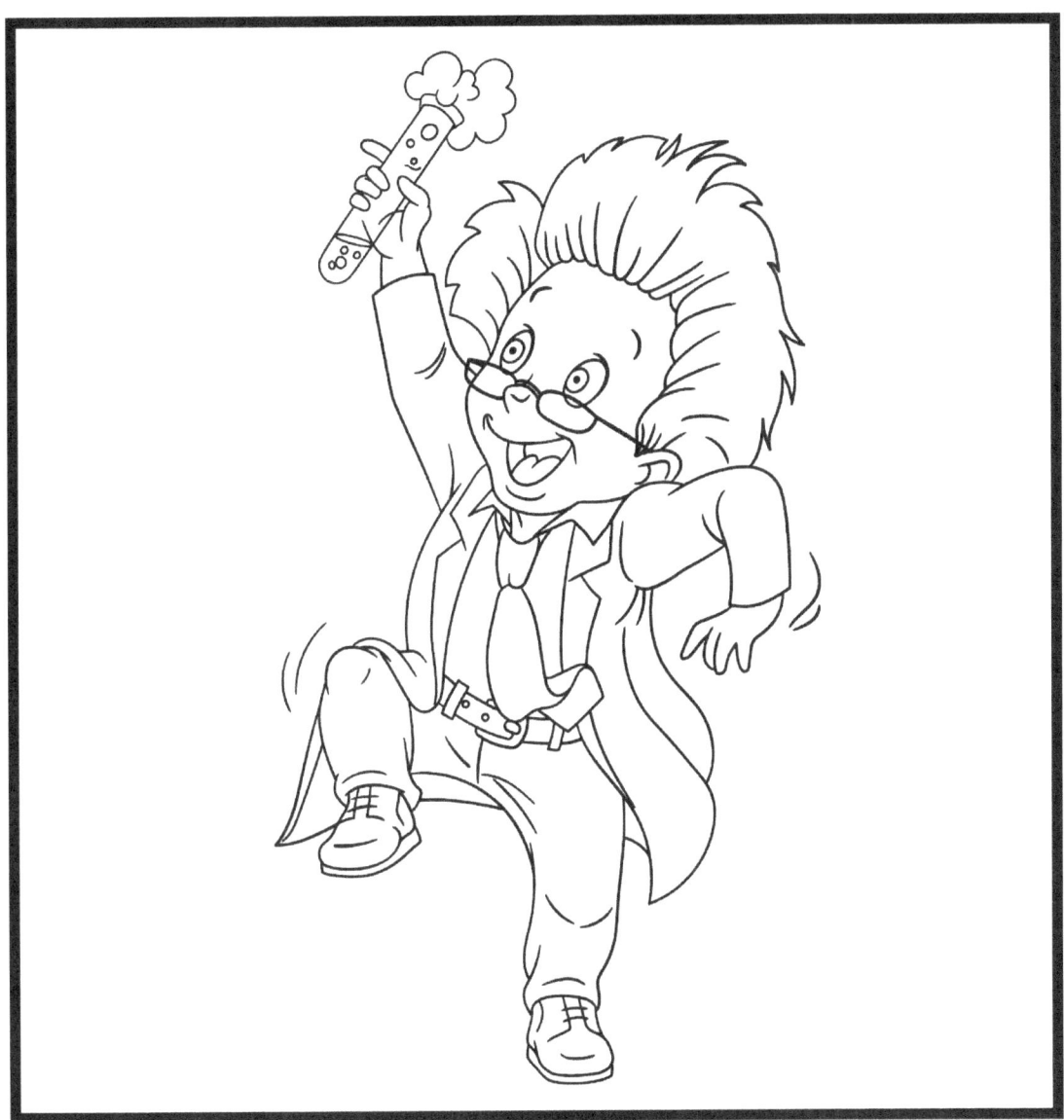

note:

_____

_____

_____

APRIL 21TH

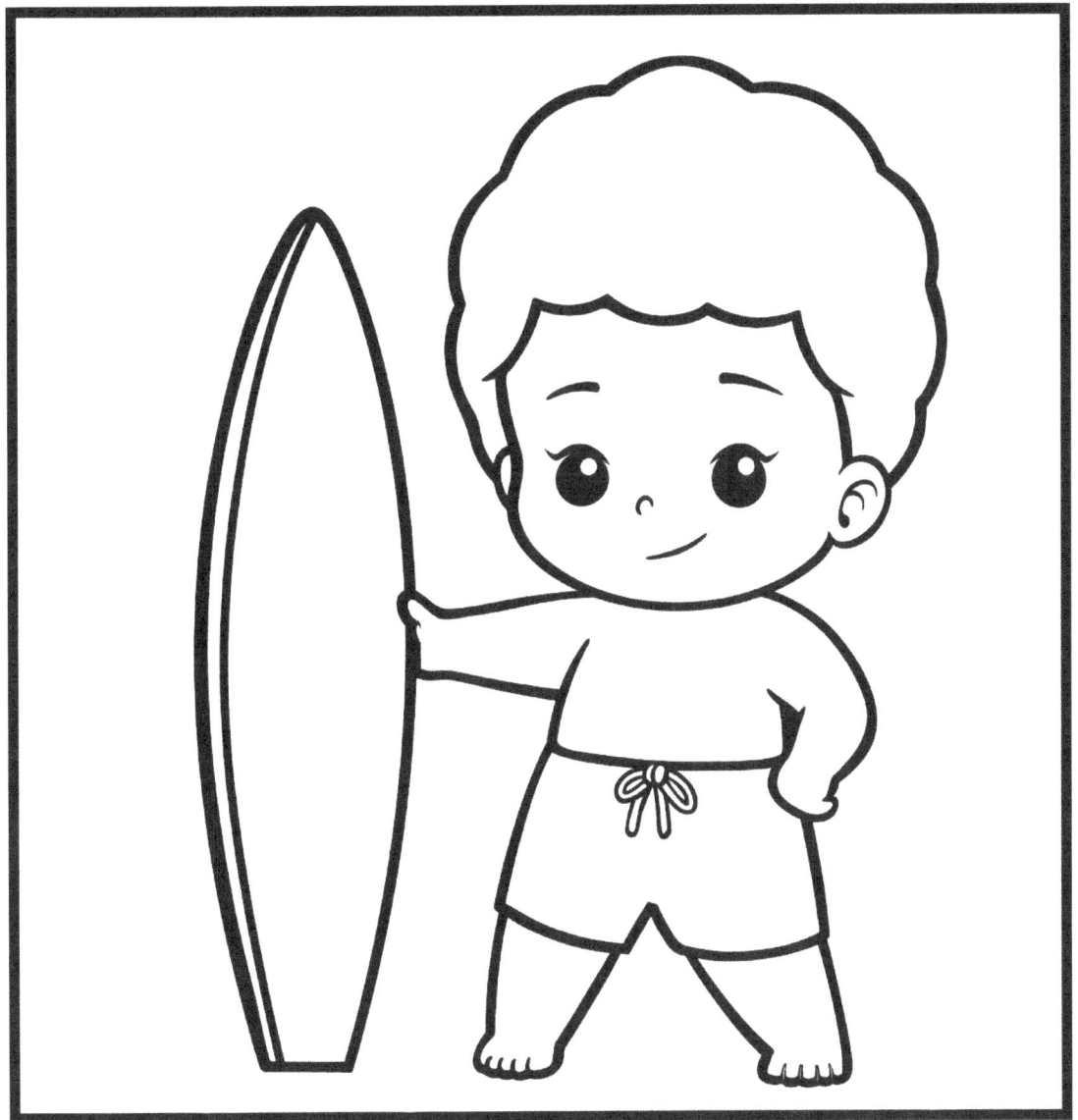

note:

_____

_____

_____

APRIL 22TH

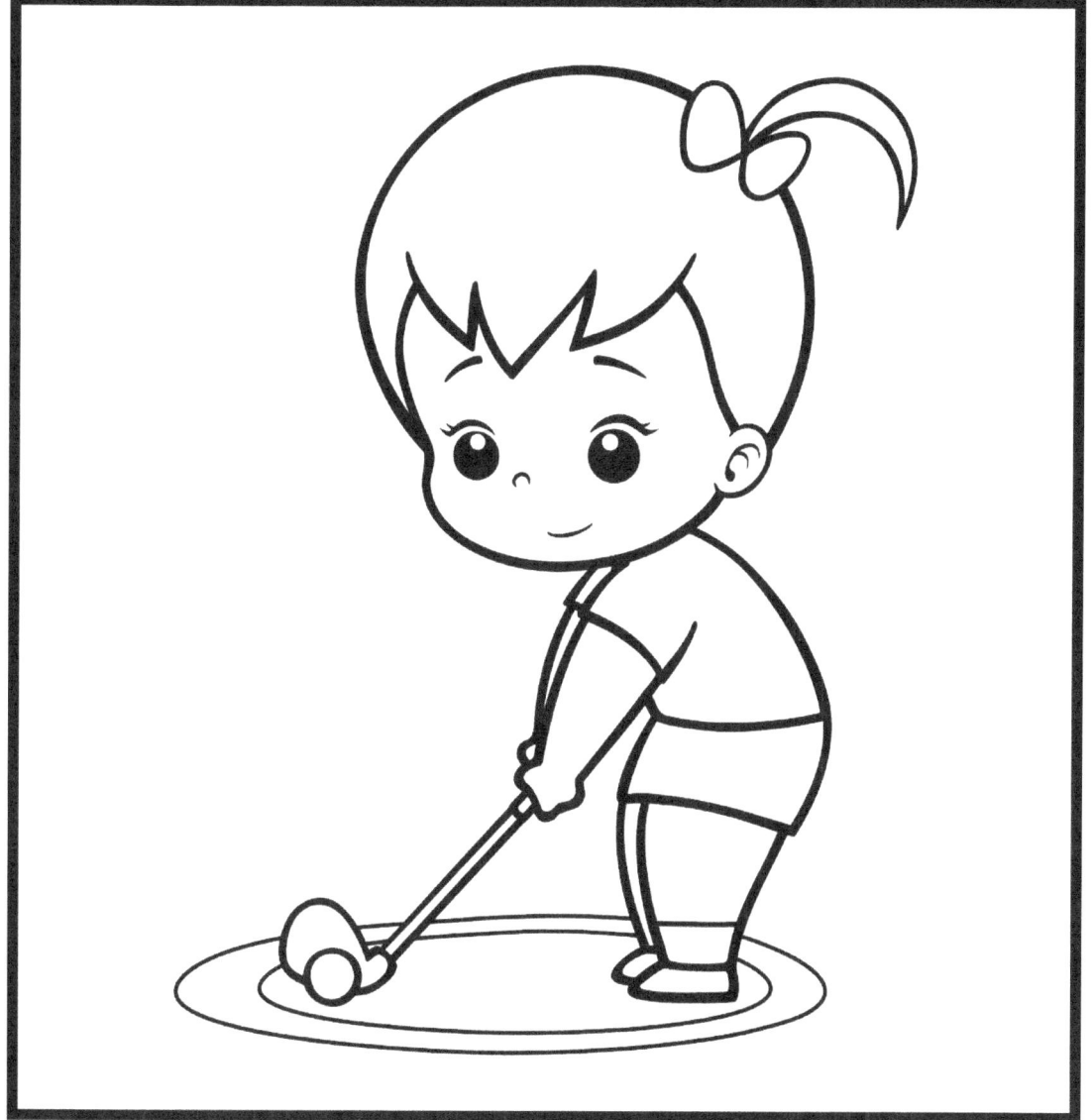

note:

_____

_____

_____

APRIL 23TH

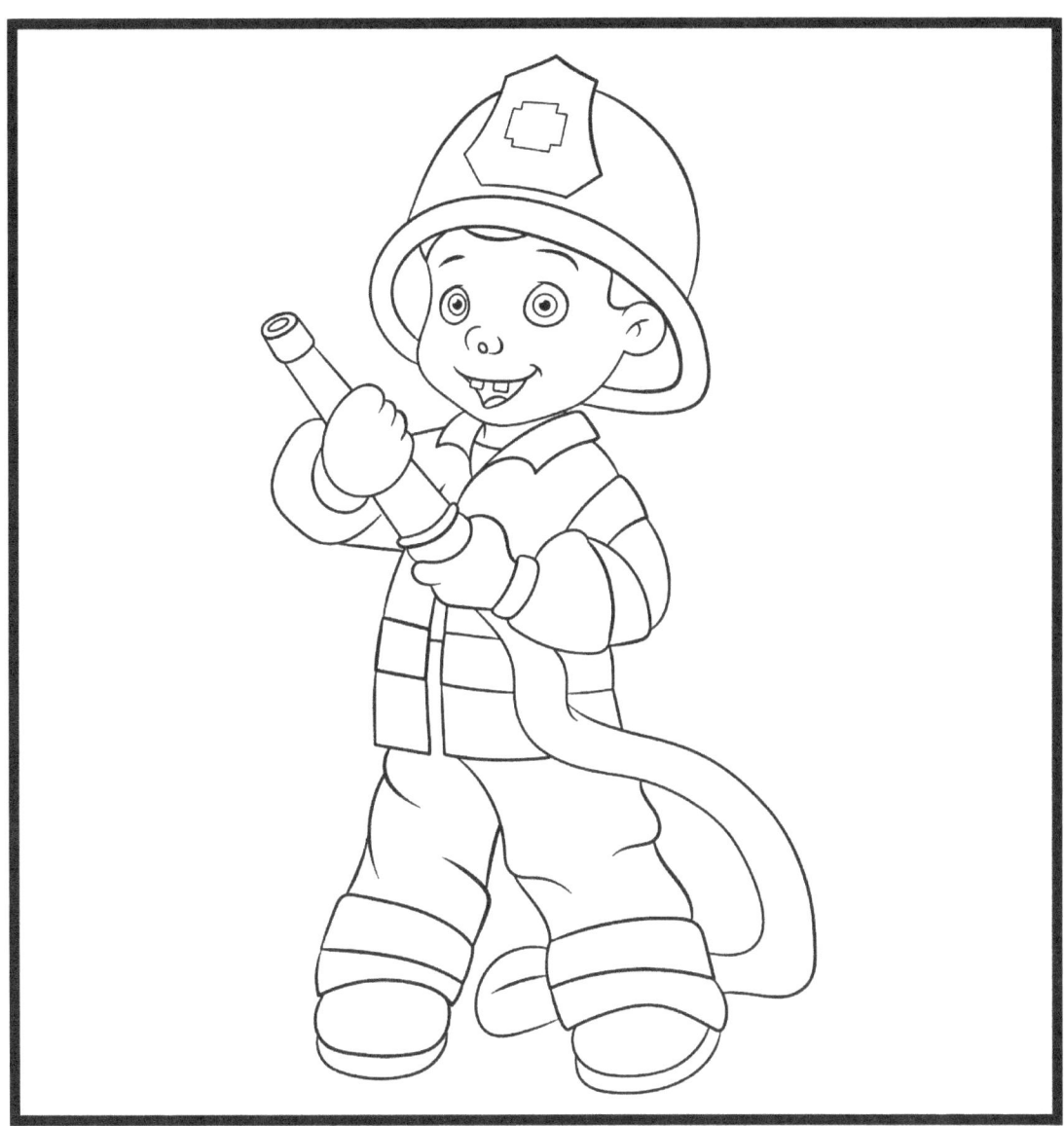

note:

_____

_____

_____

APRIL 24TH

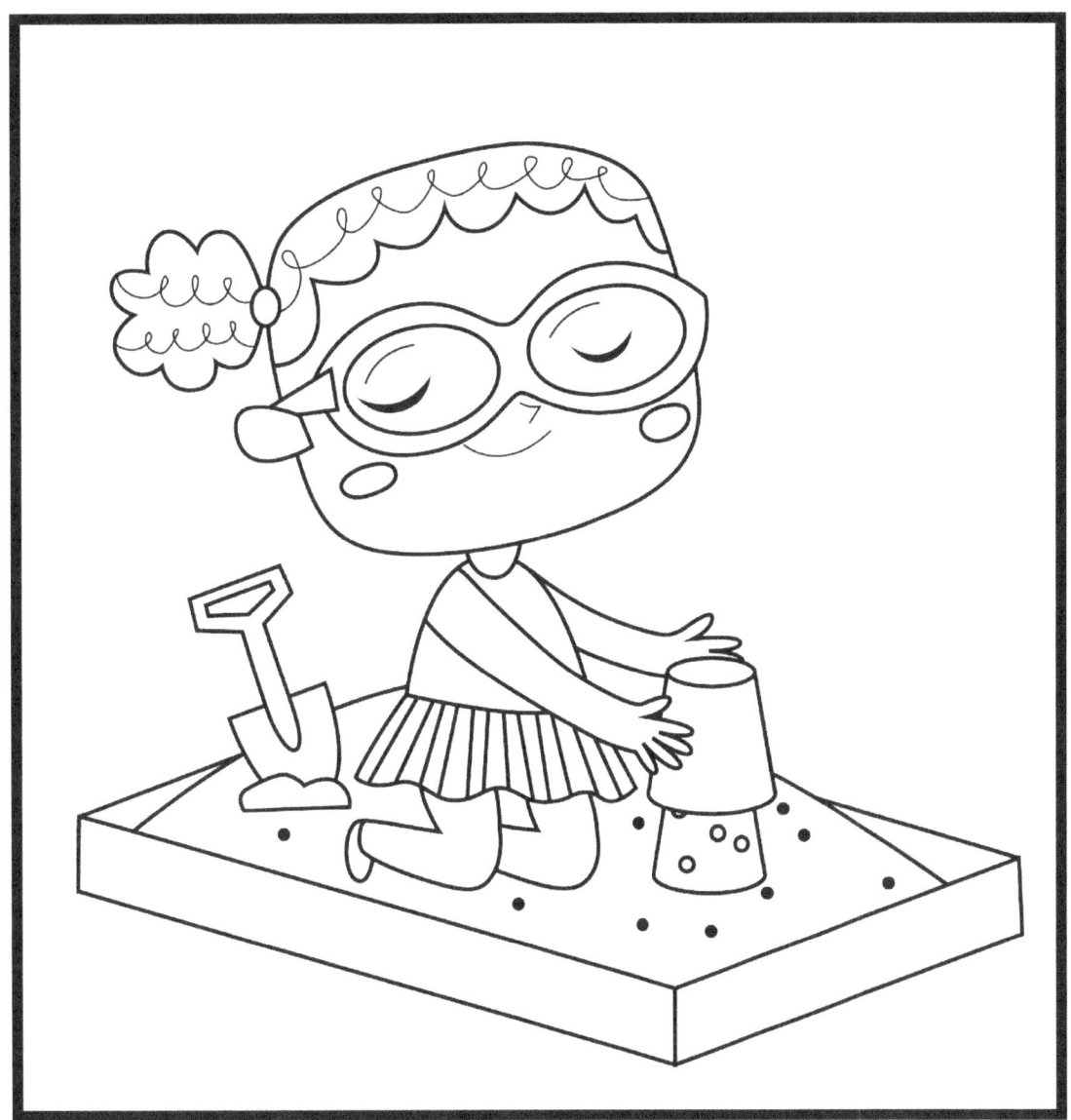

note:

_____

_____

_____

APRIL 25TH

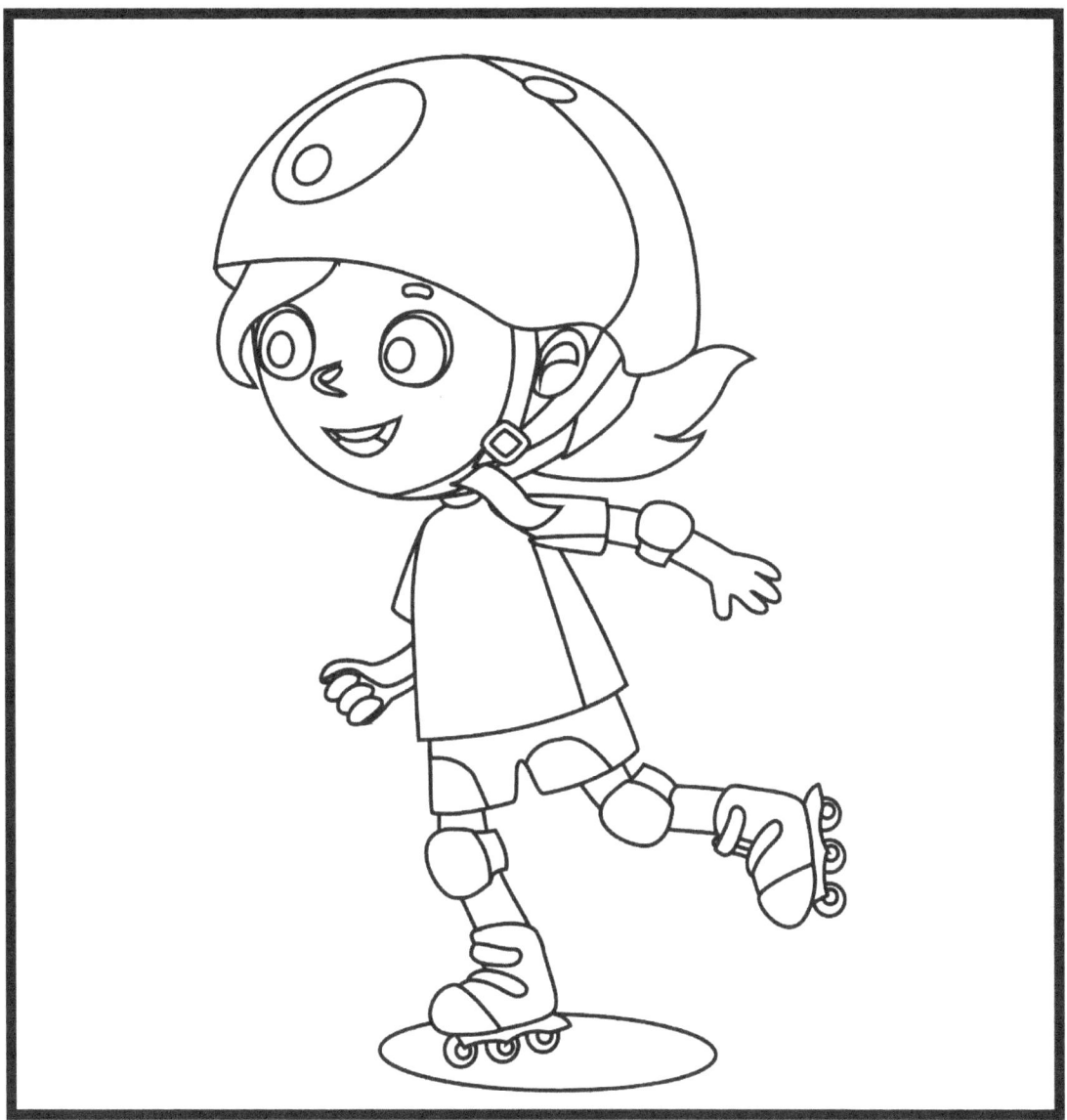

note:

_____

_____

_____

APRIL 26TH

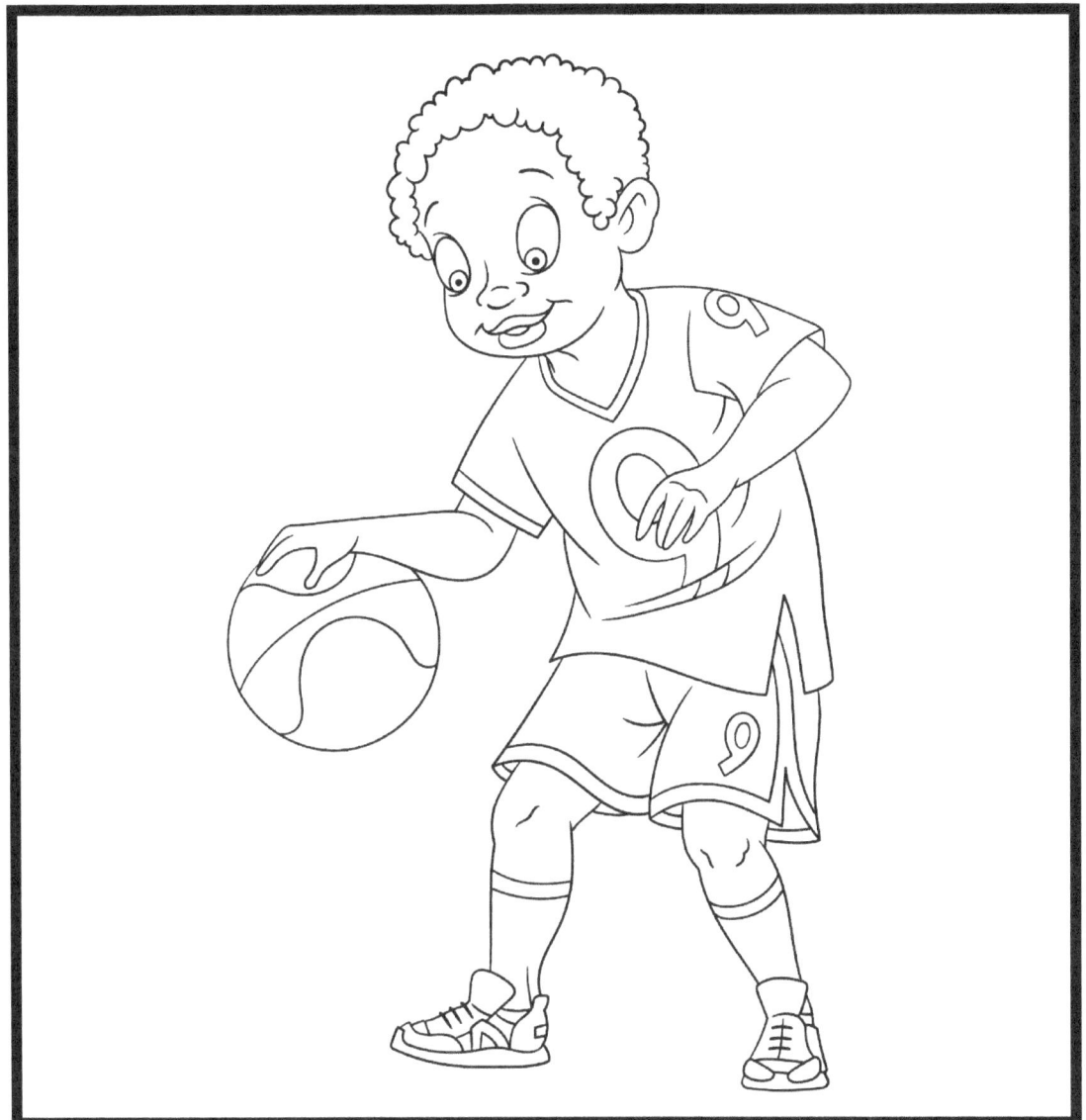

note:

_____

_____

_____

APRIL 27TH

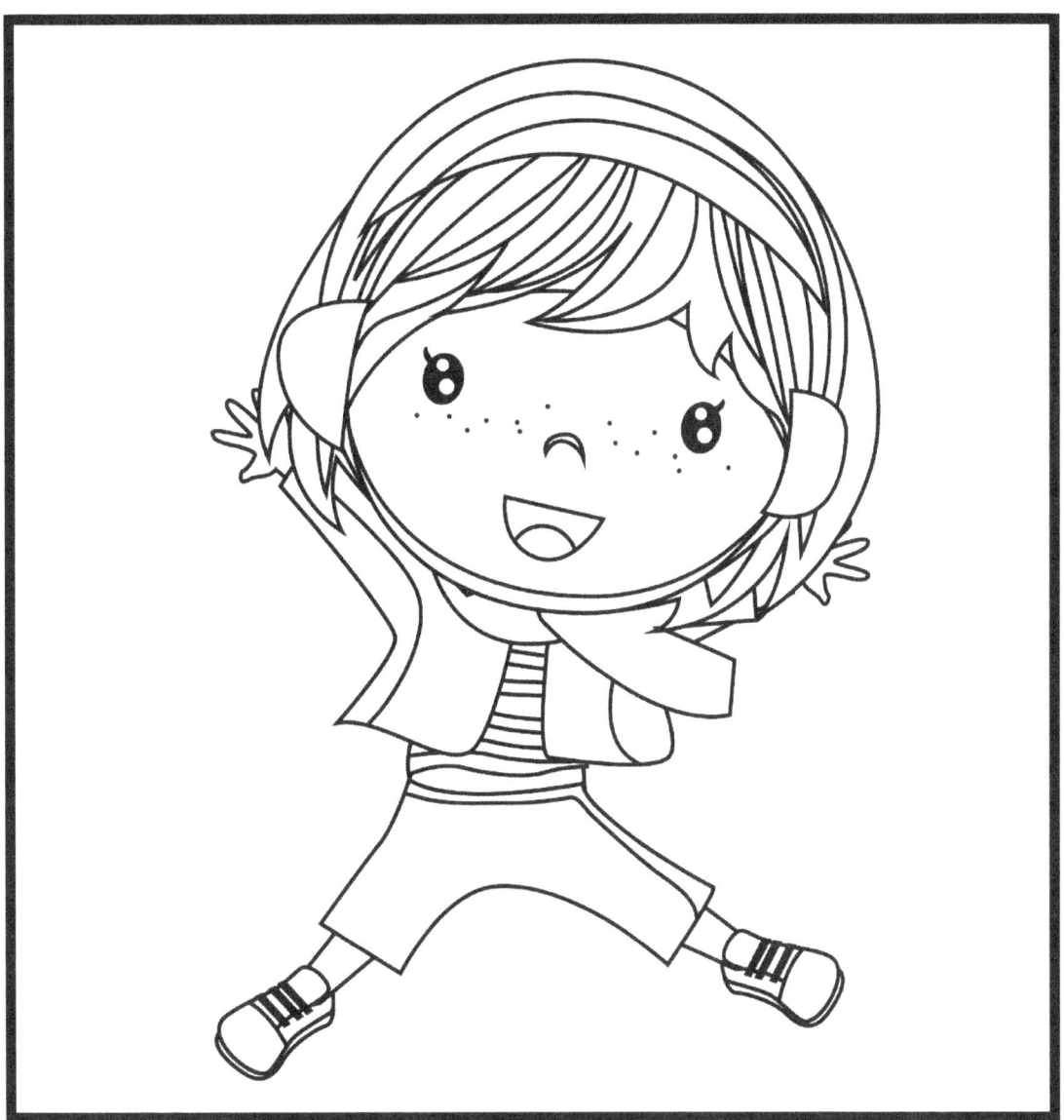

note:

_____

_____

_____

APRIL 28TH

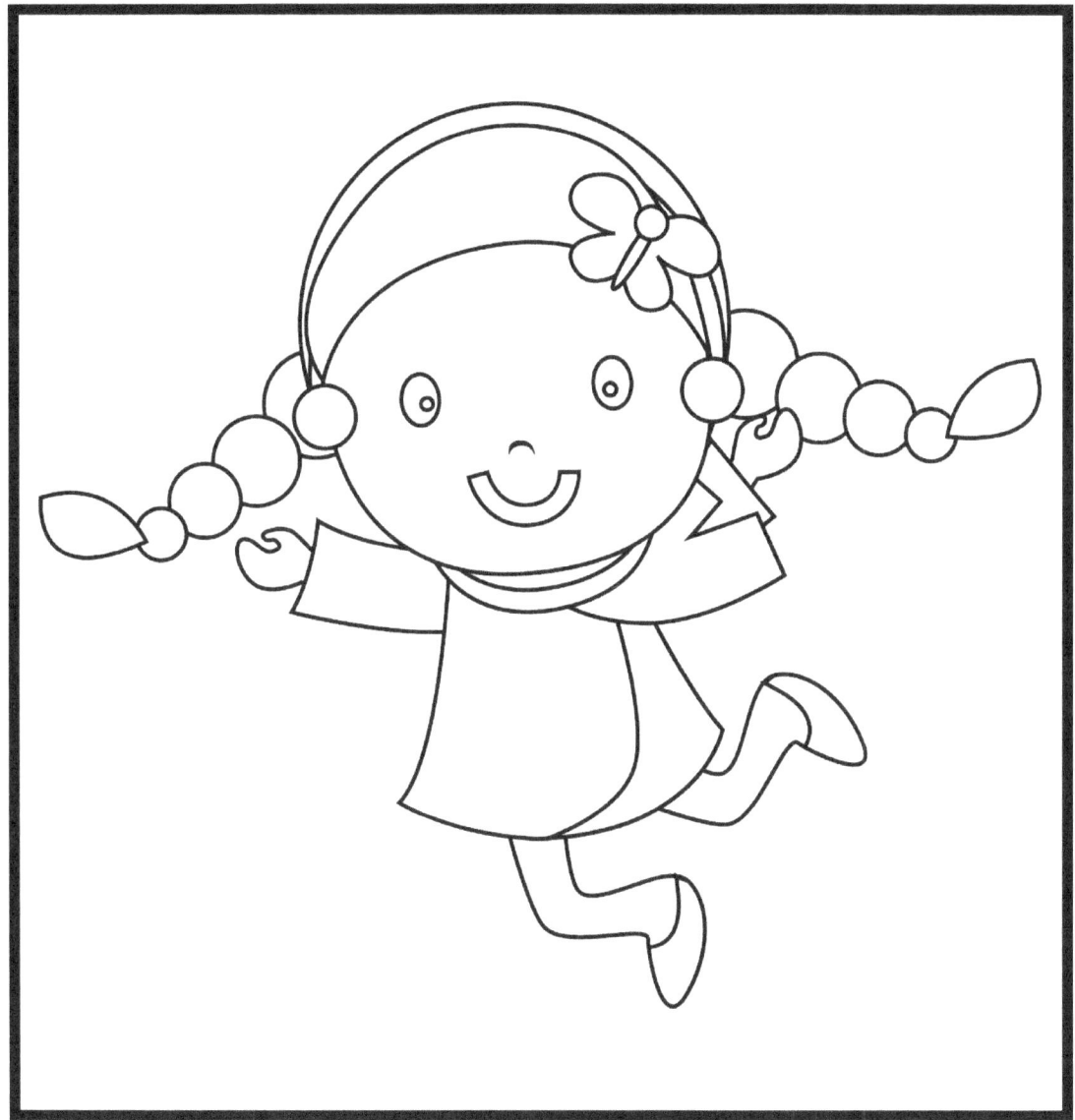

note:

_____

_____

_____

APRIL 29TH

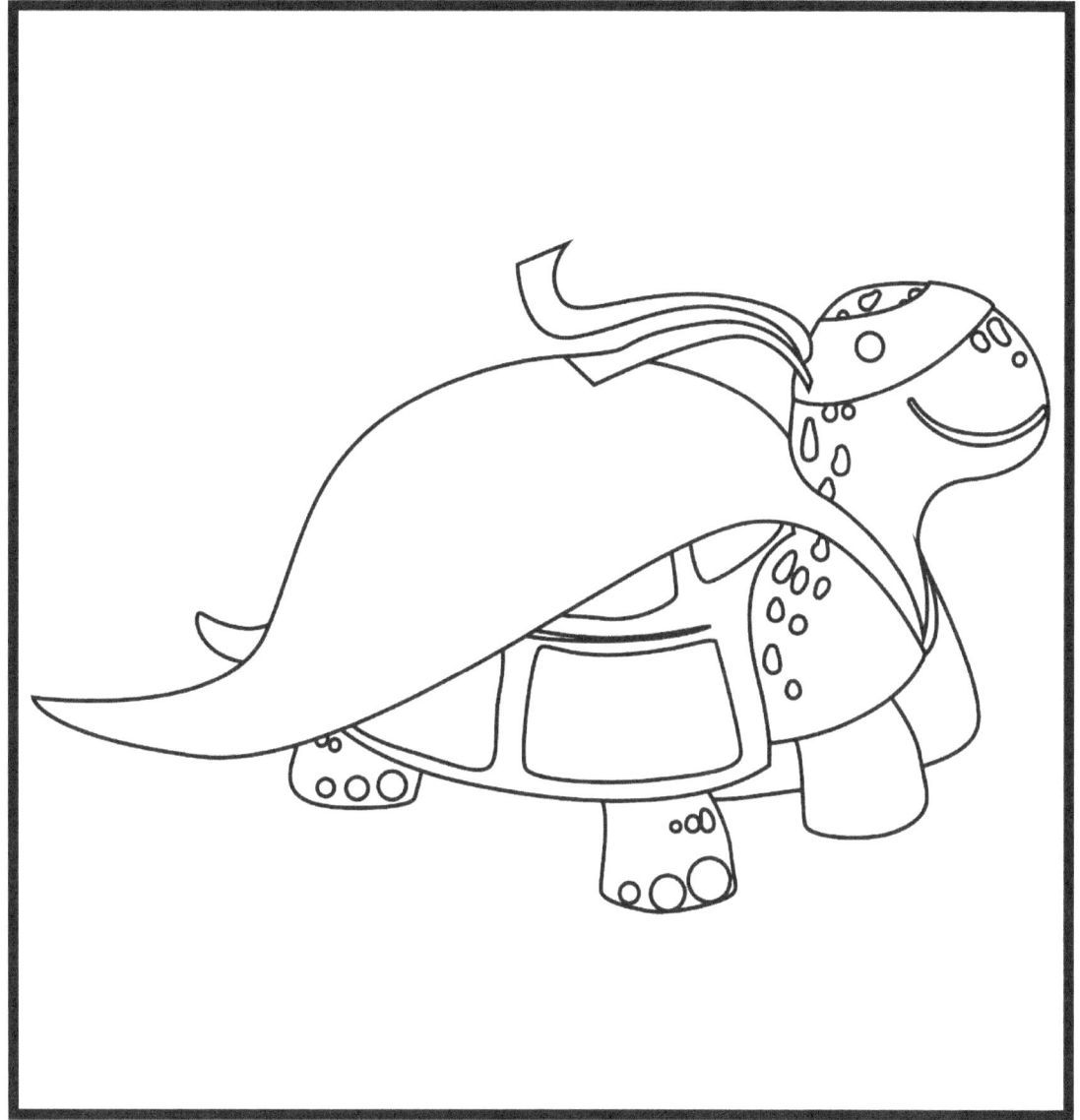

note:

_____

_____

_____

APRIL 30TH

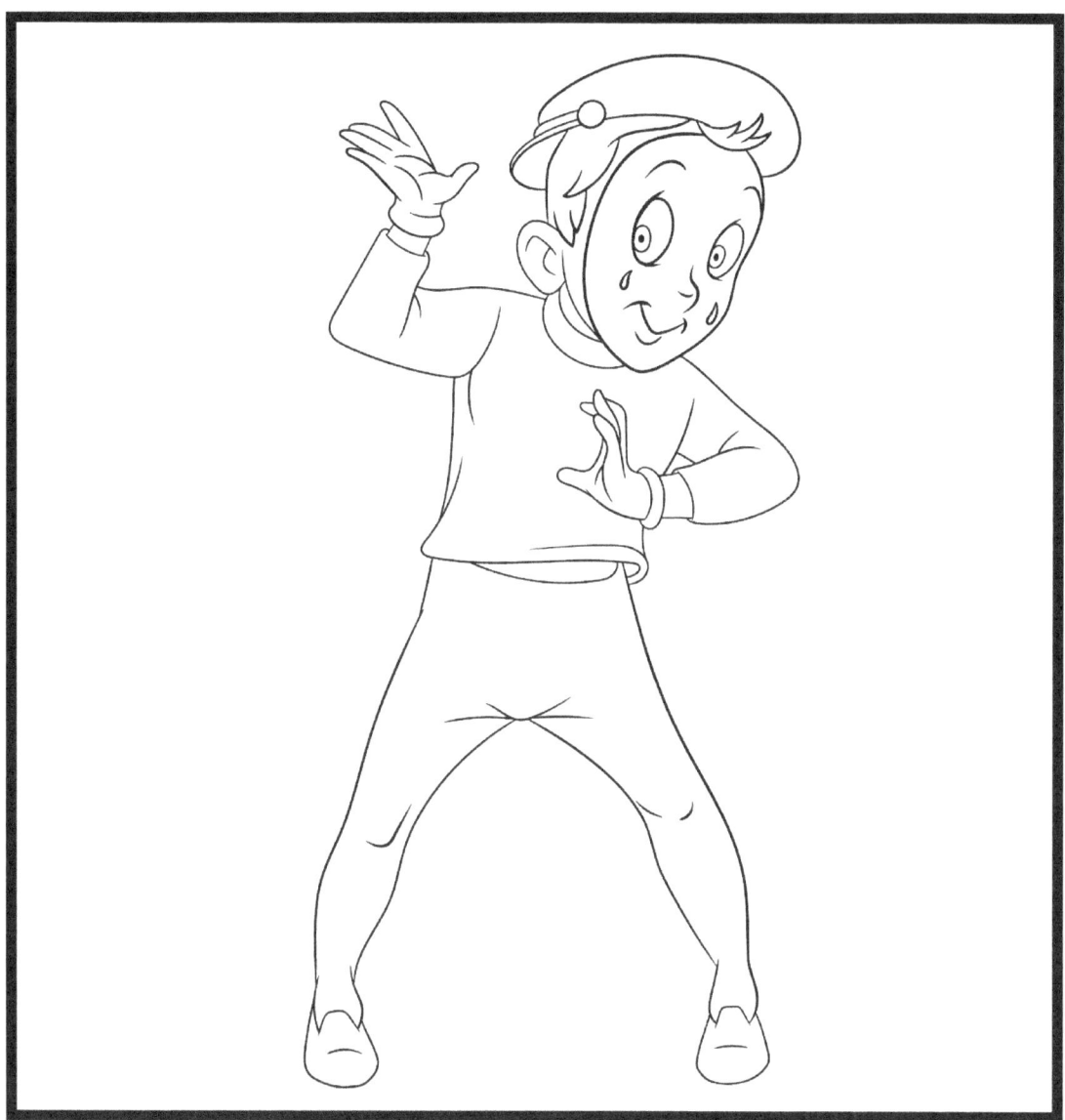

note:

_____

_____

_____

APRIL 31TH

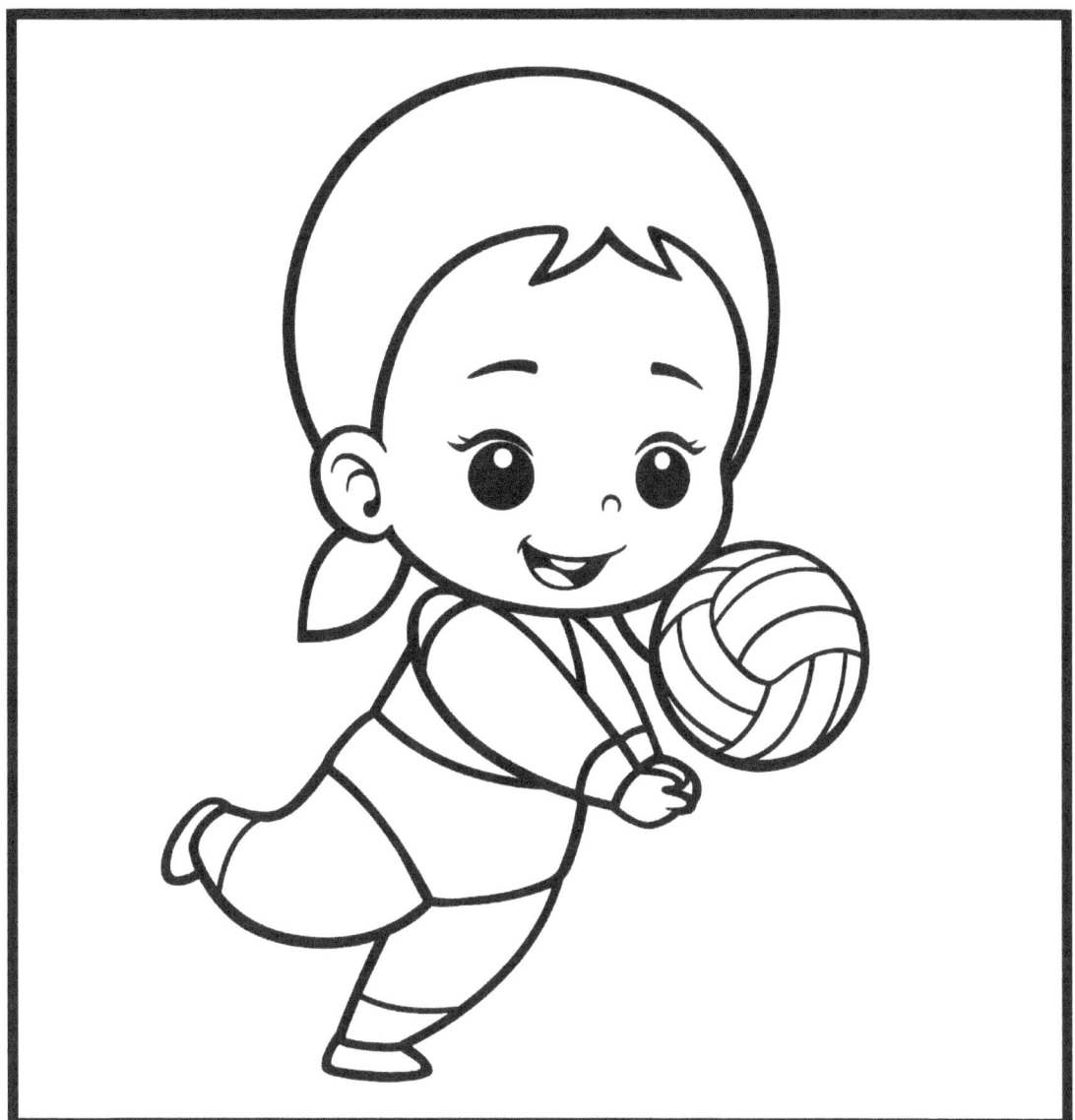

note:

_____

_____

_____

APRIL 32TH

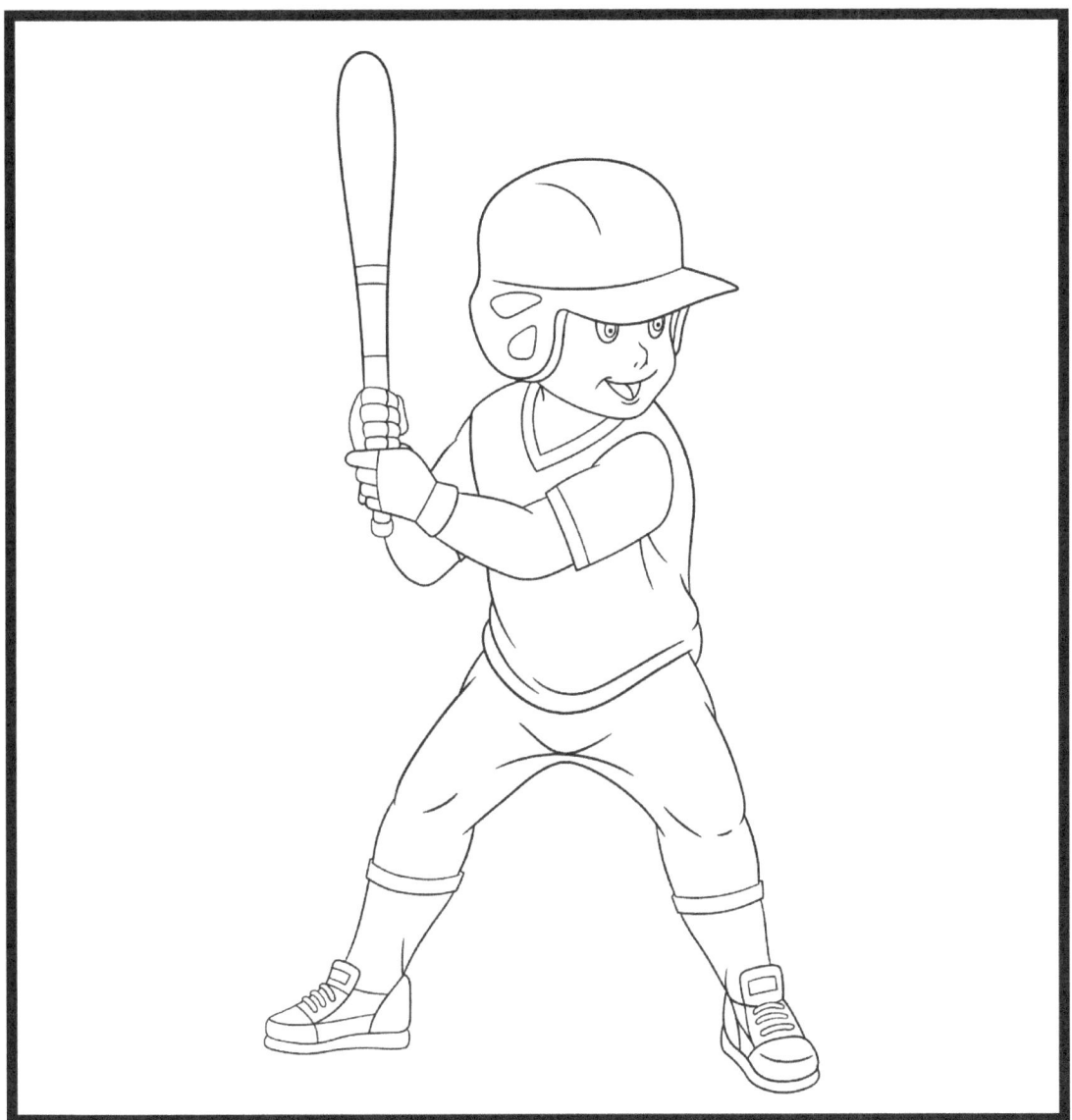

note:

_____

_____

_____

APRIL 33TH

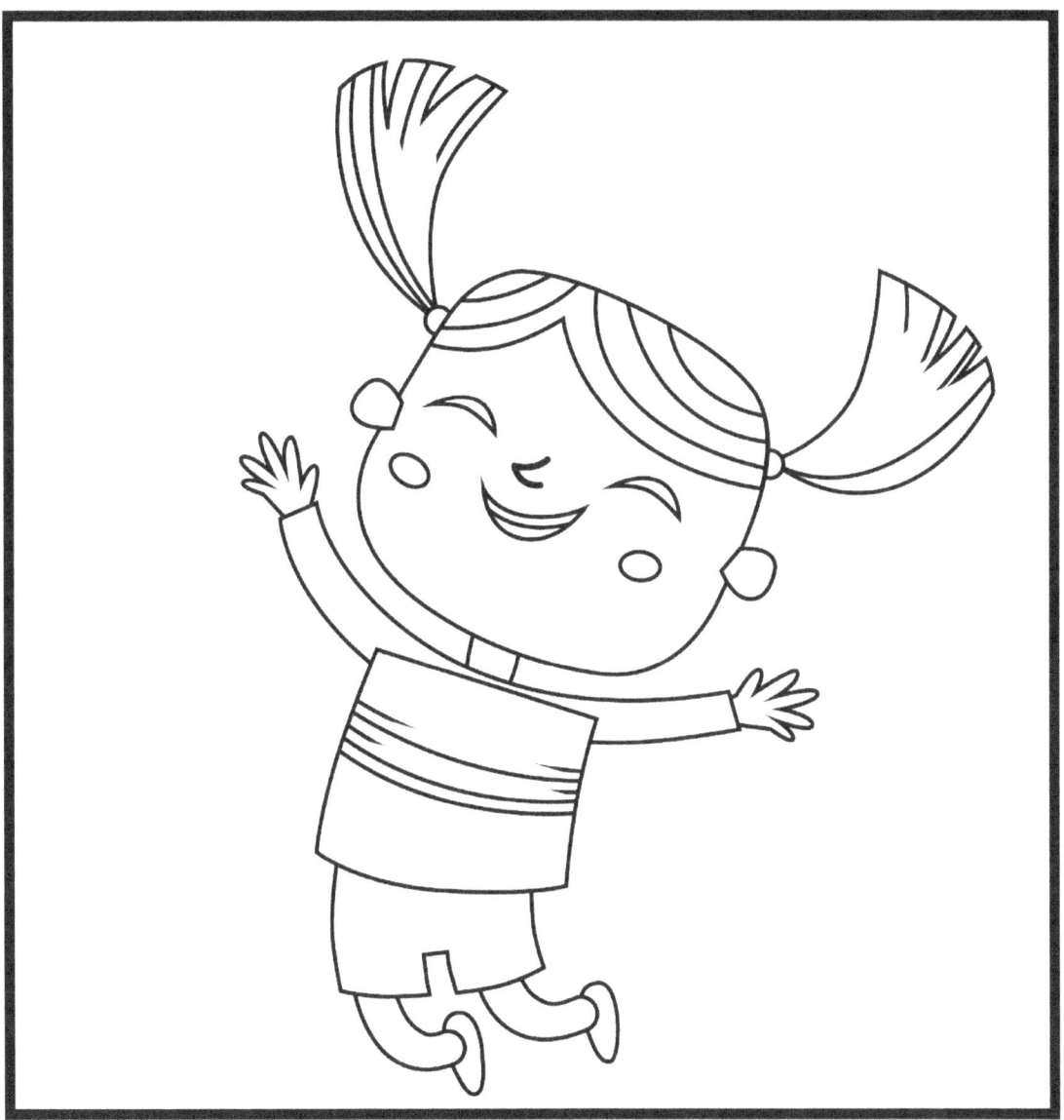

note:

_____

_____

_____

APRIL 34TH

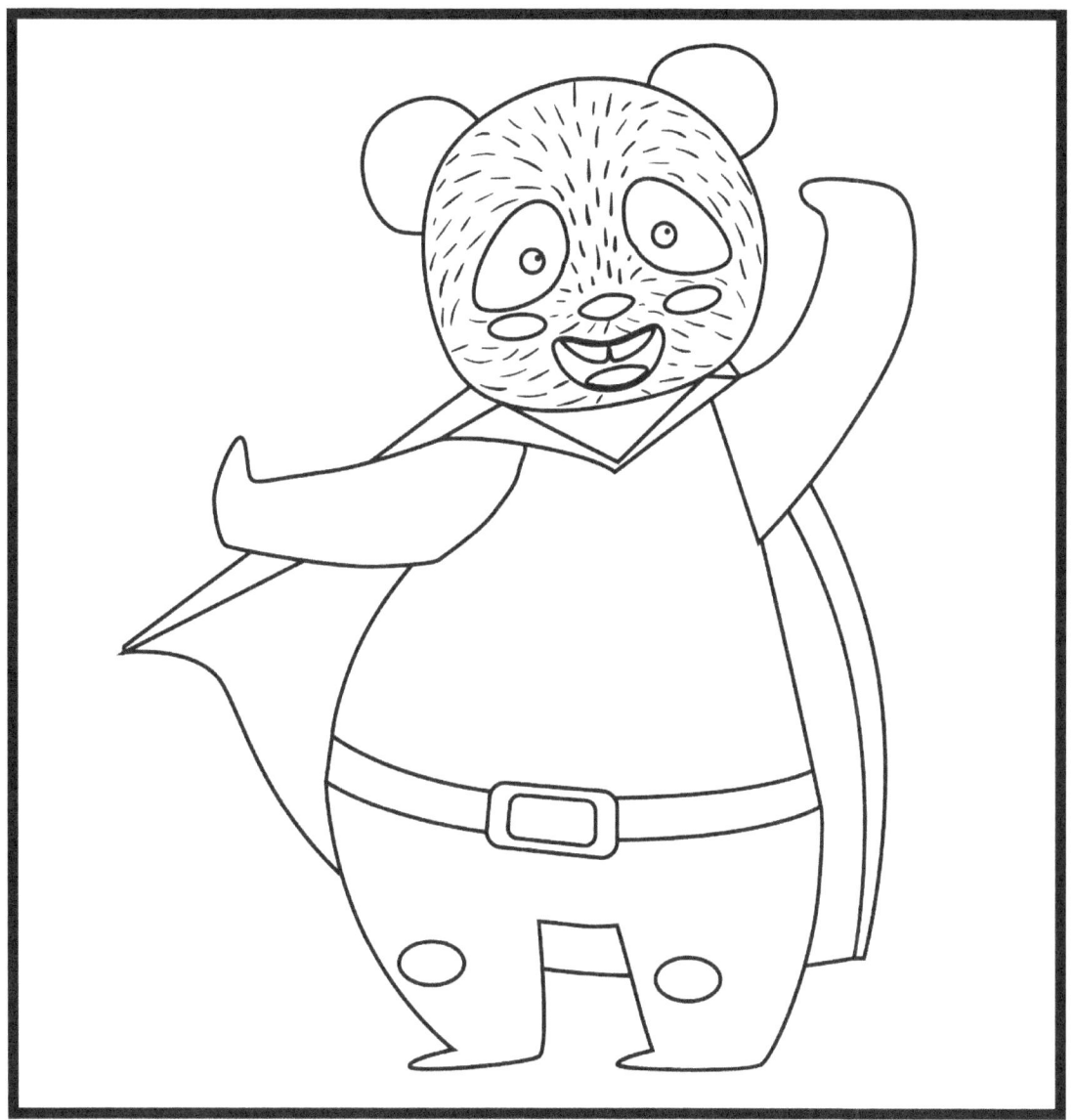

note:

_____

_____

_____

APRIL 35TH

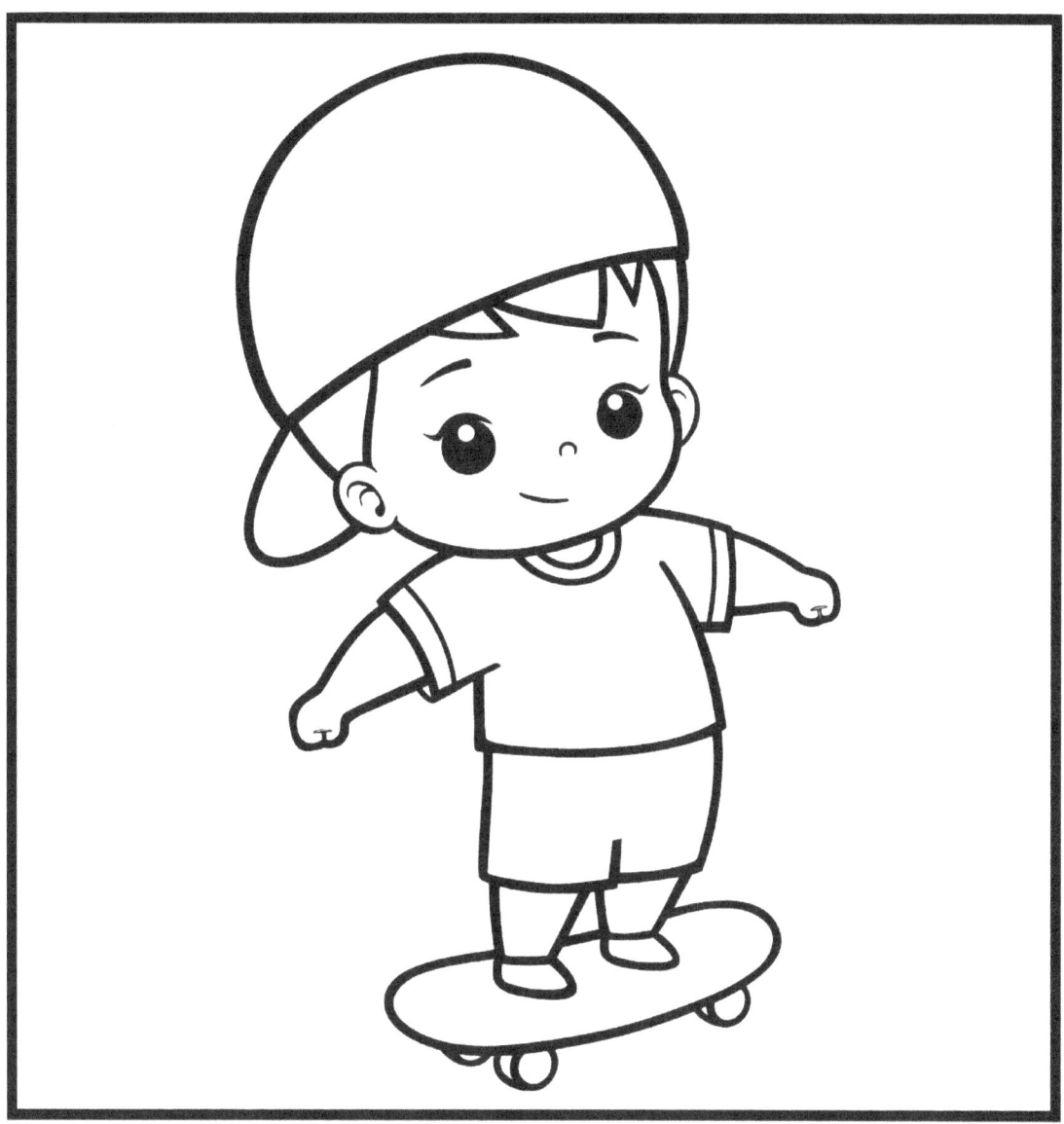

note:

_____

_____

_____

APRIL 36TH

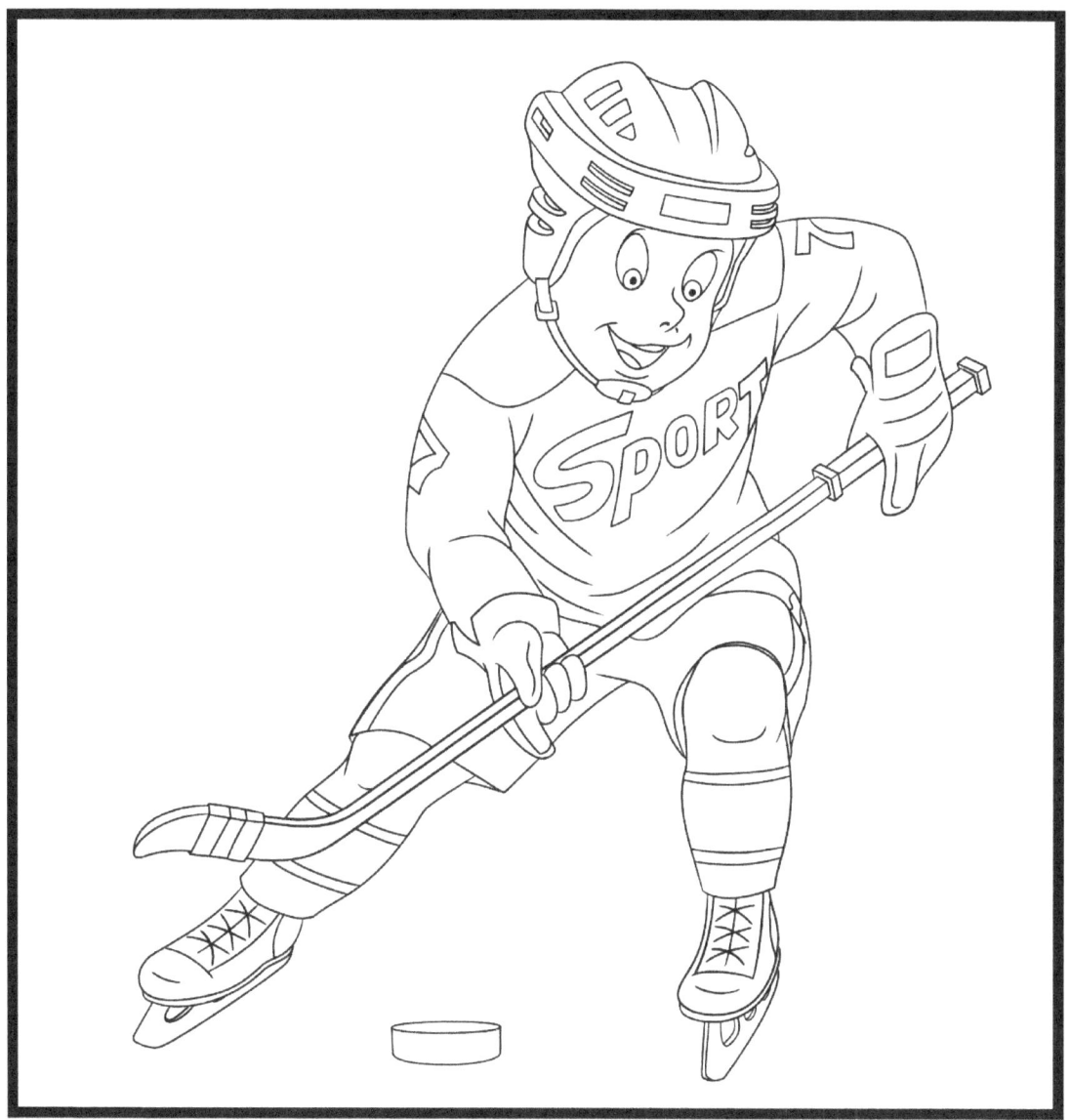

note:

_____

_____

_____

APRIL 37TH

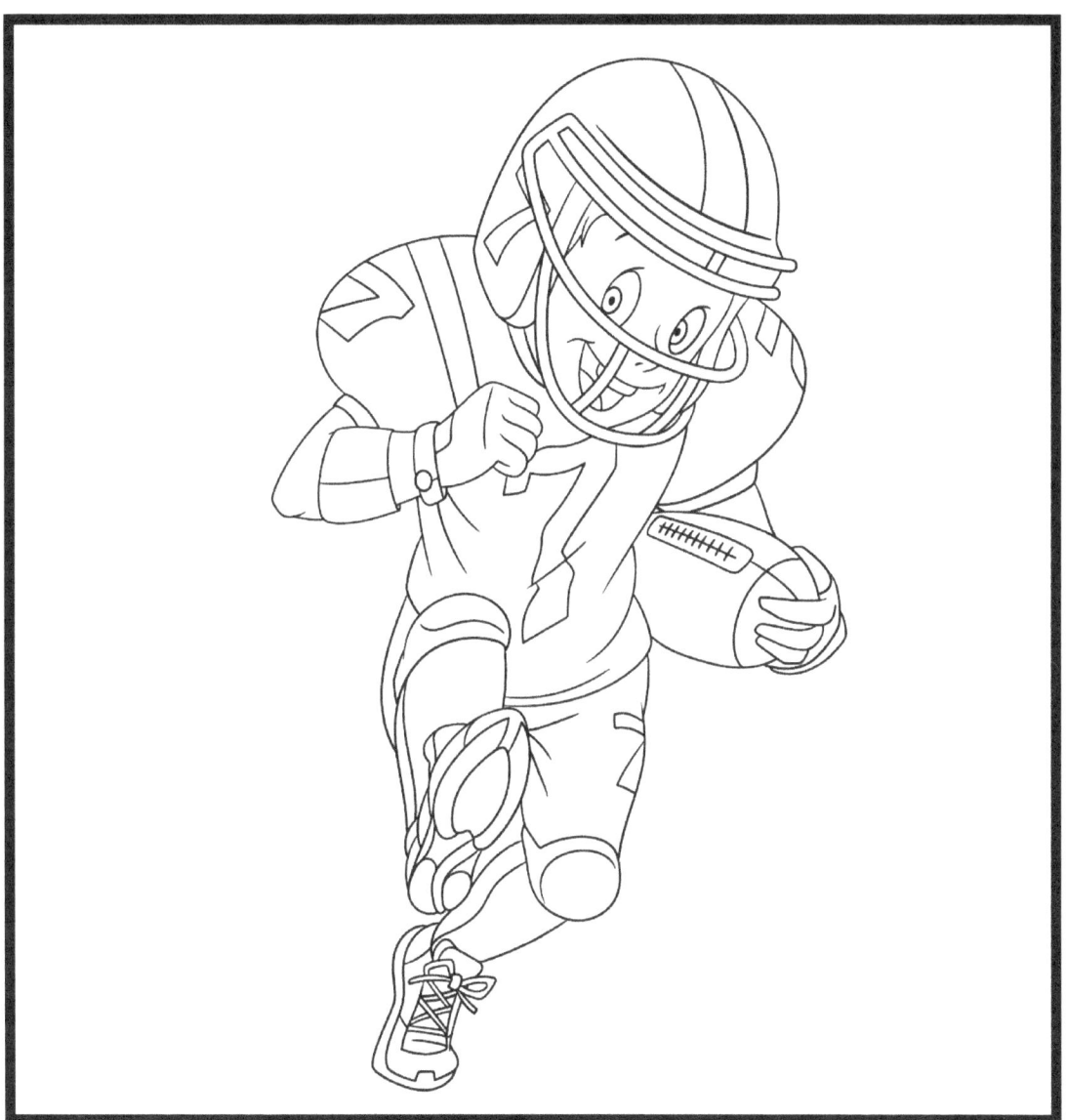

note:

_____

_____

_____

APRIL 38TH

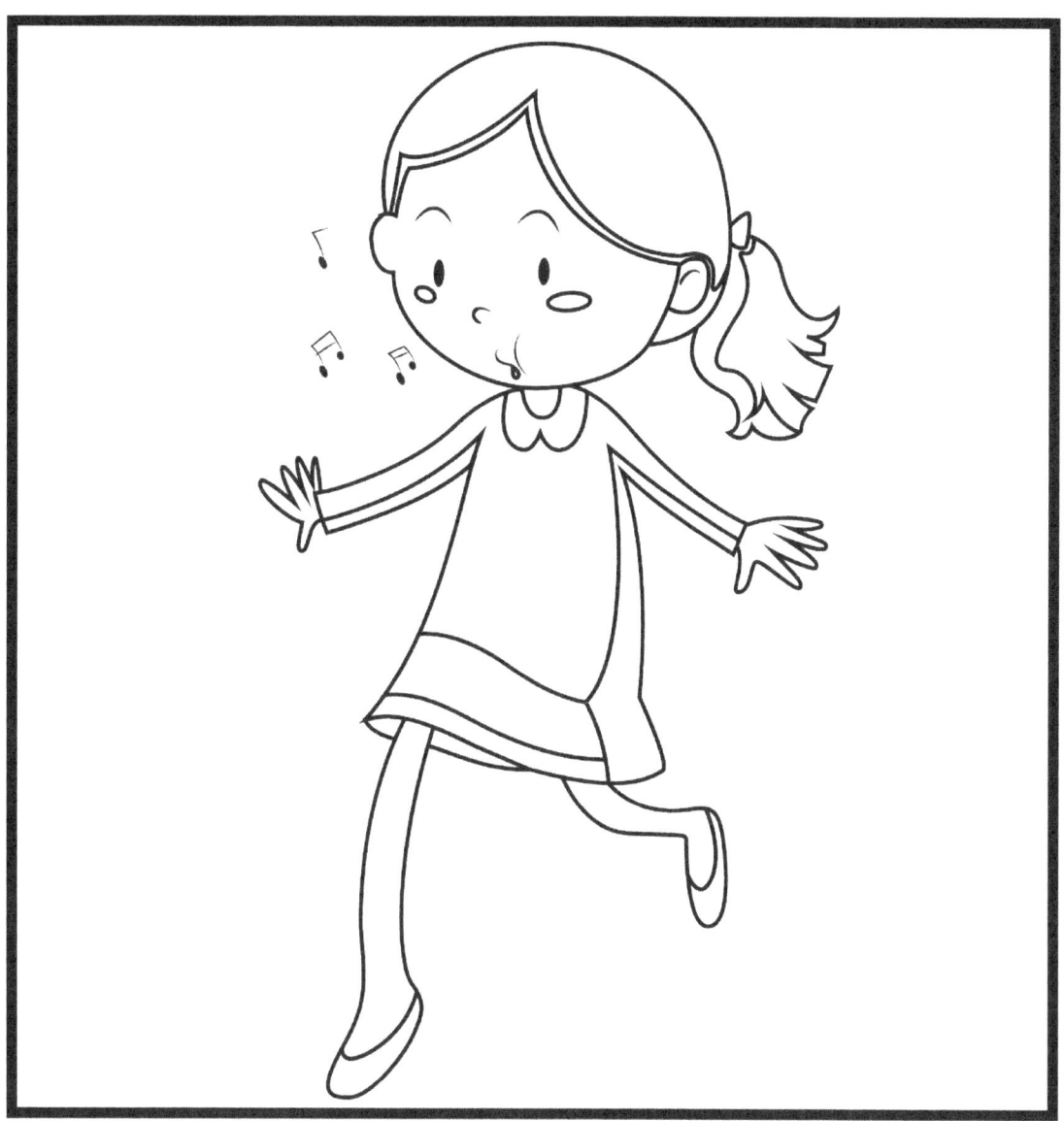

note:

_____

_____

_____

APRIL 39TH

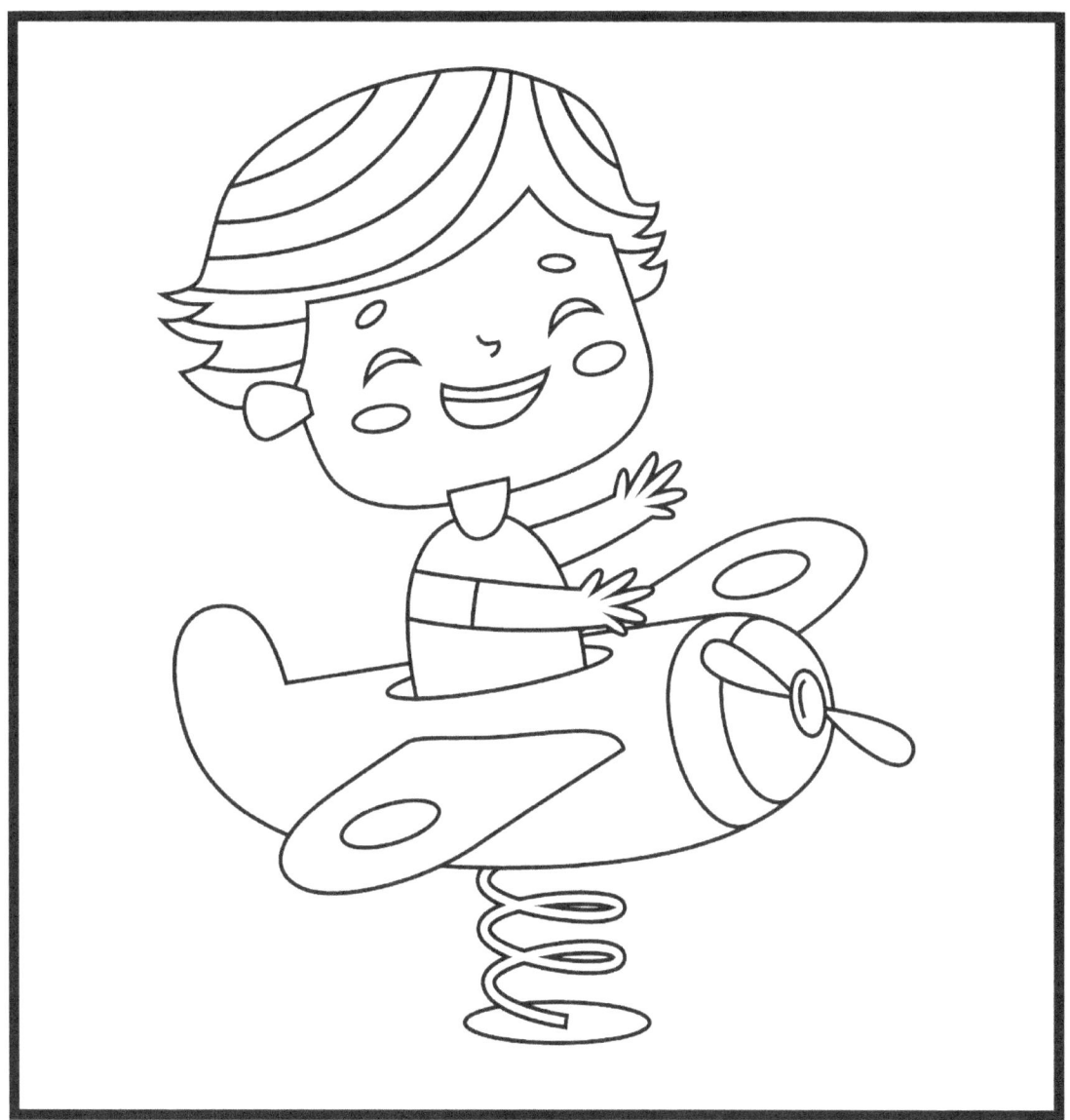

note:

_____

_____

_____

APRIL 40TH

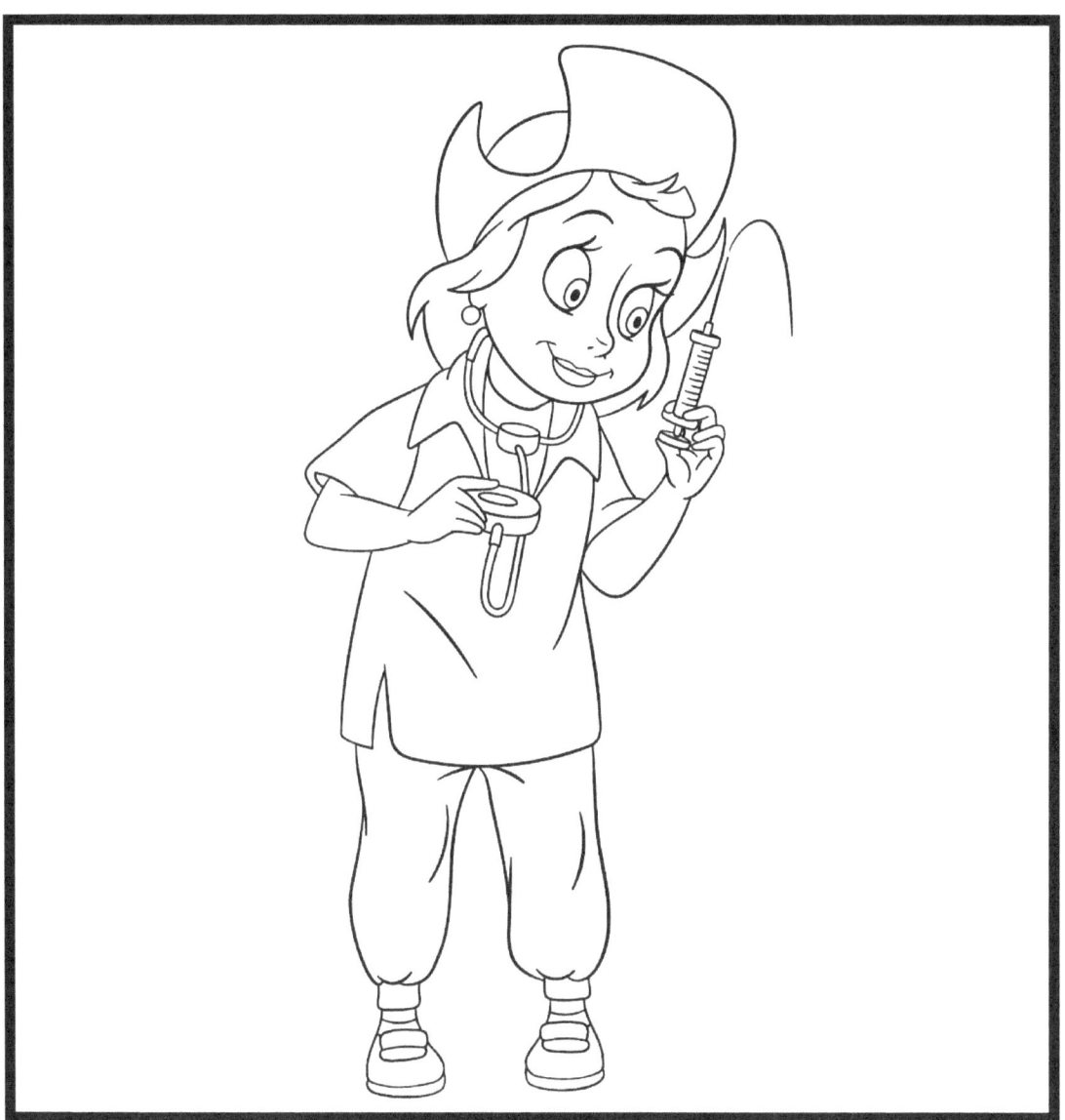

note:

_____

_____

_____

APRIL 41TH

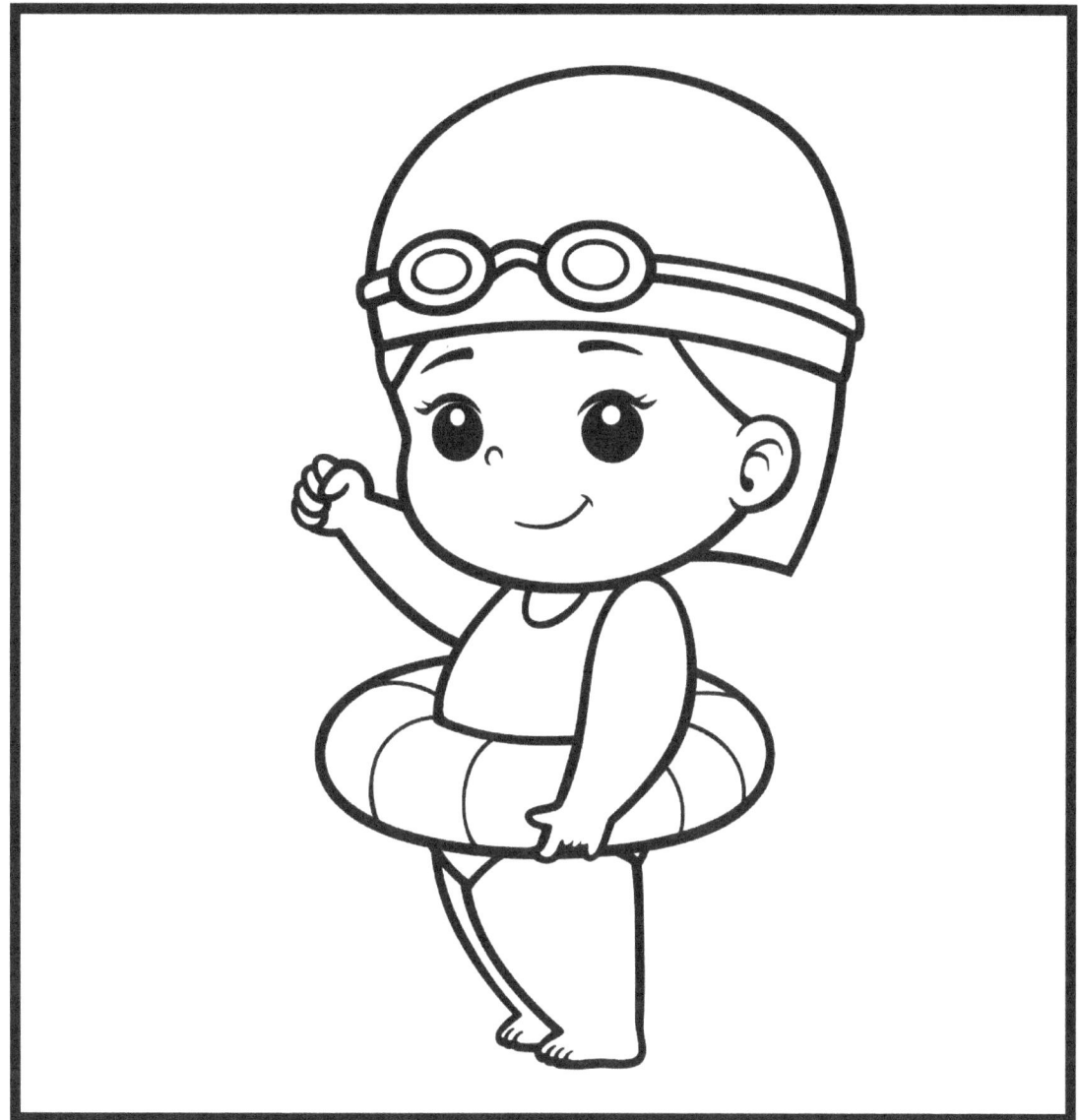

note:

_____

_____

_____

APRIL 42TH

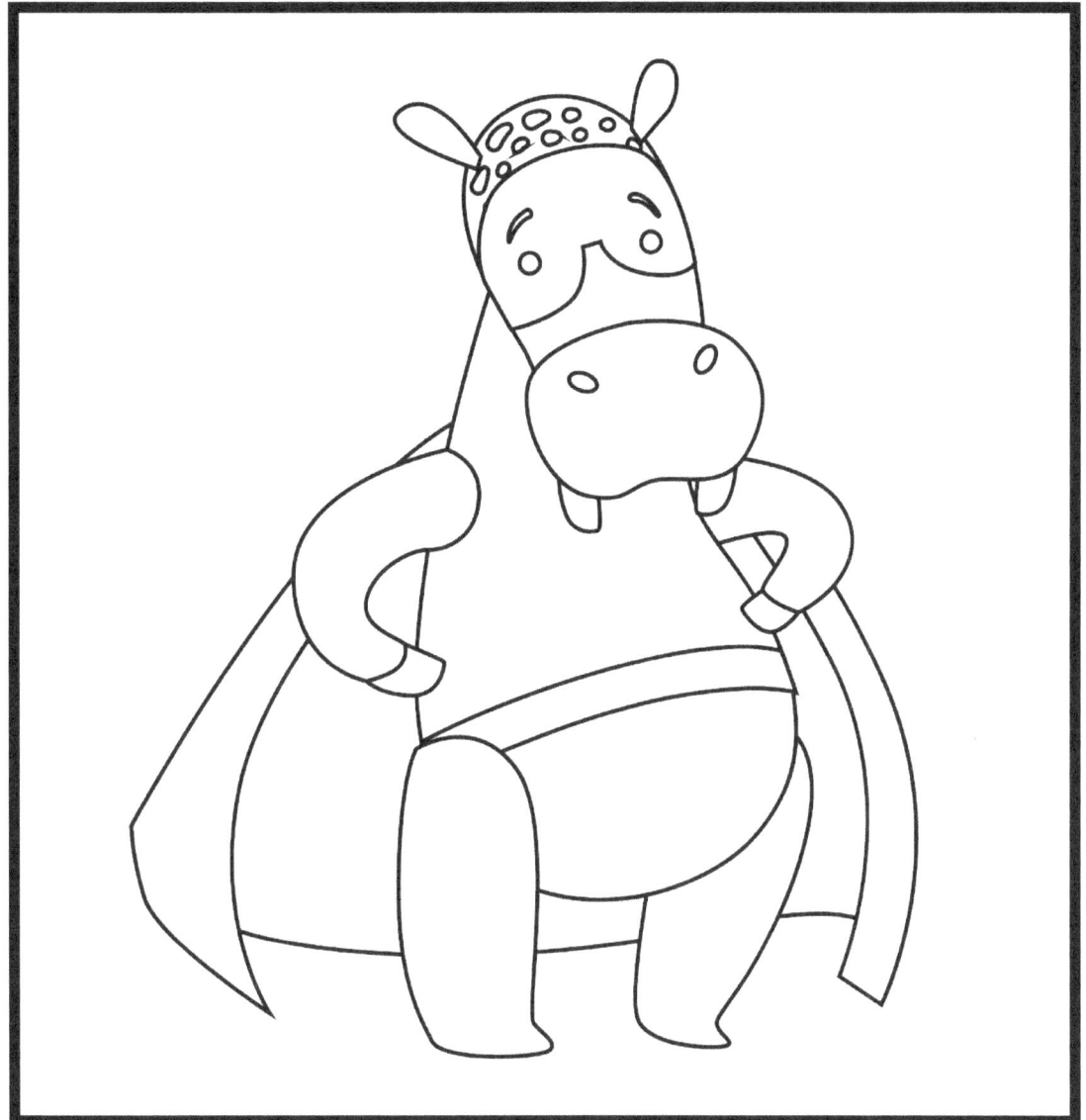

note:

_____

_____

_____

APRIL 43TH

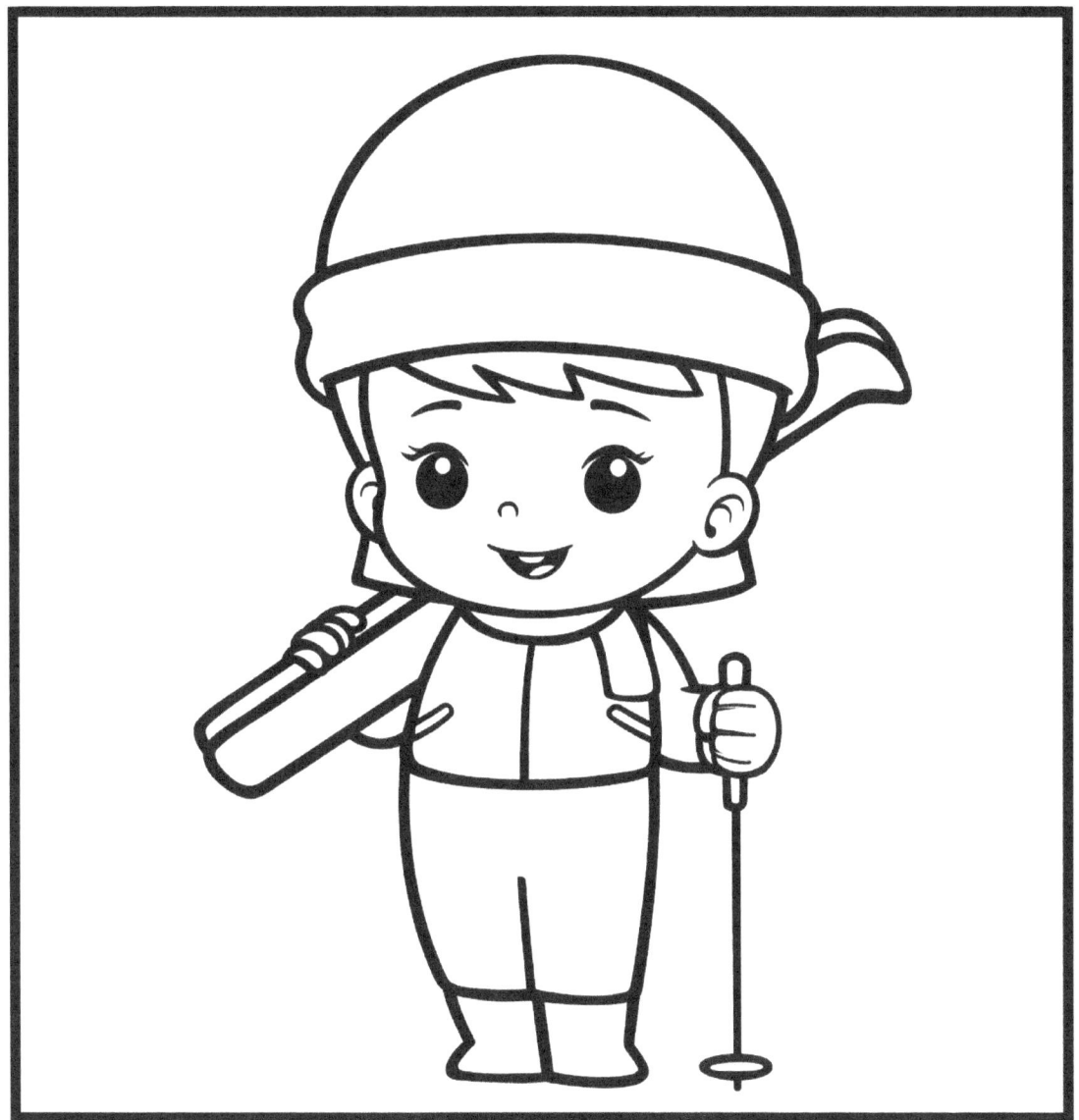

note:

_____

_____

_____

APRIL 44TH

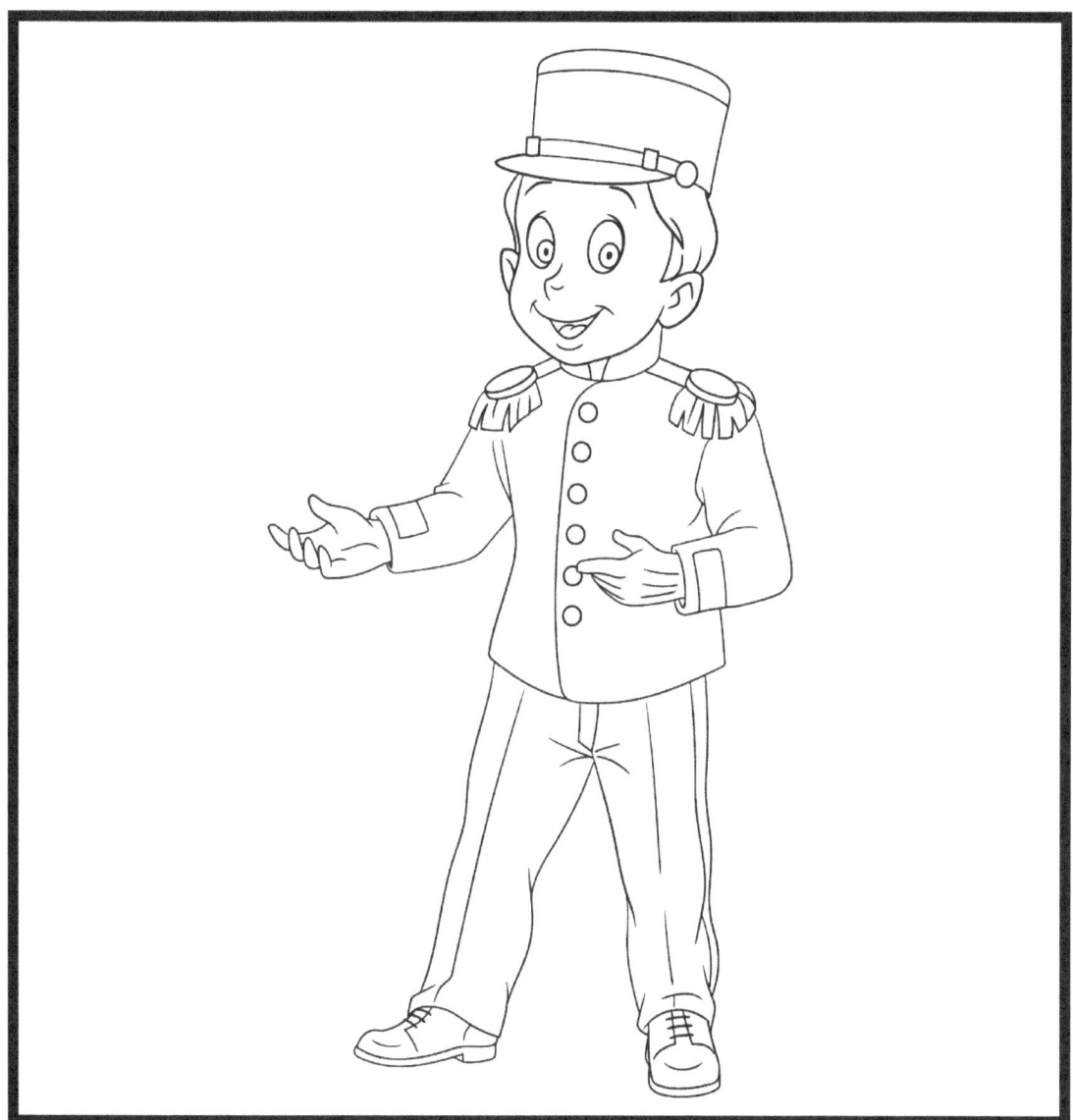

note:

_____

_____

_____

APRIL 45TH

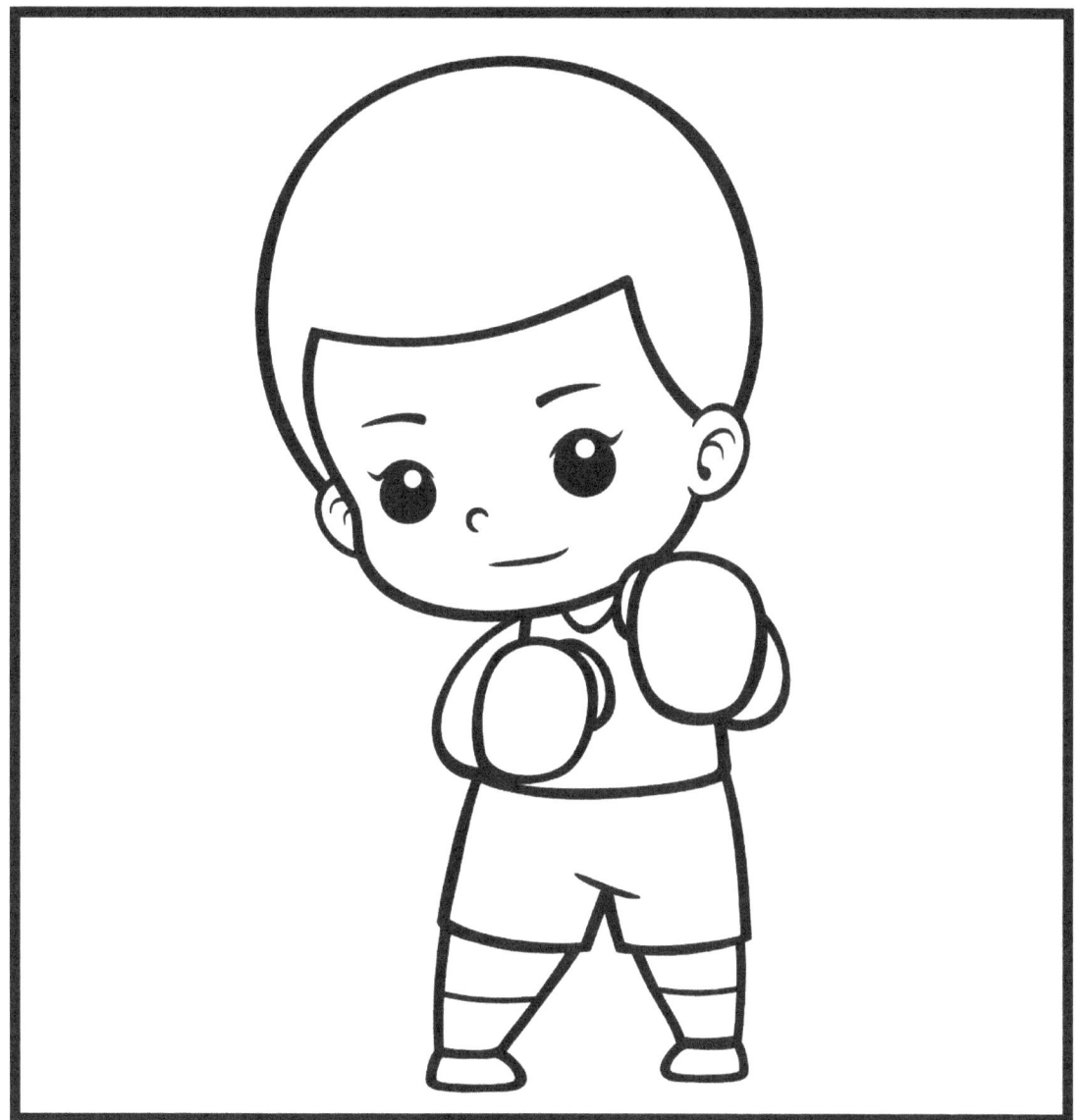

note:

_____

_____

_____

APRIL 46TH

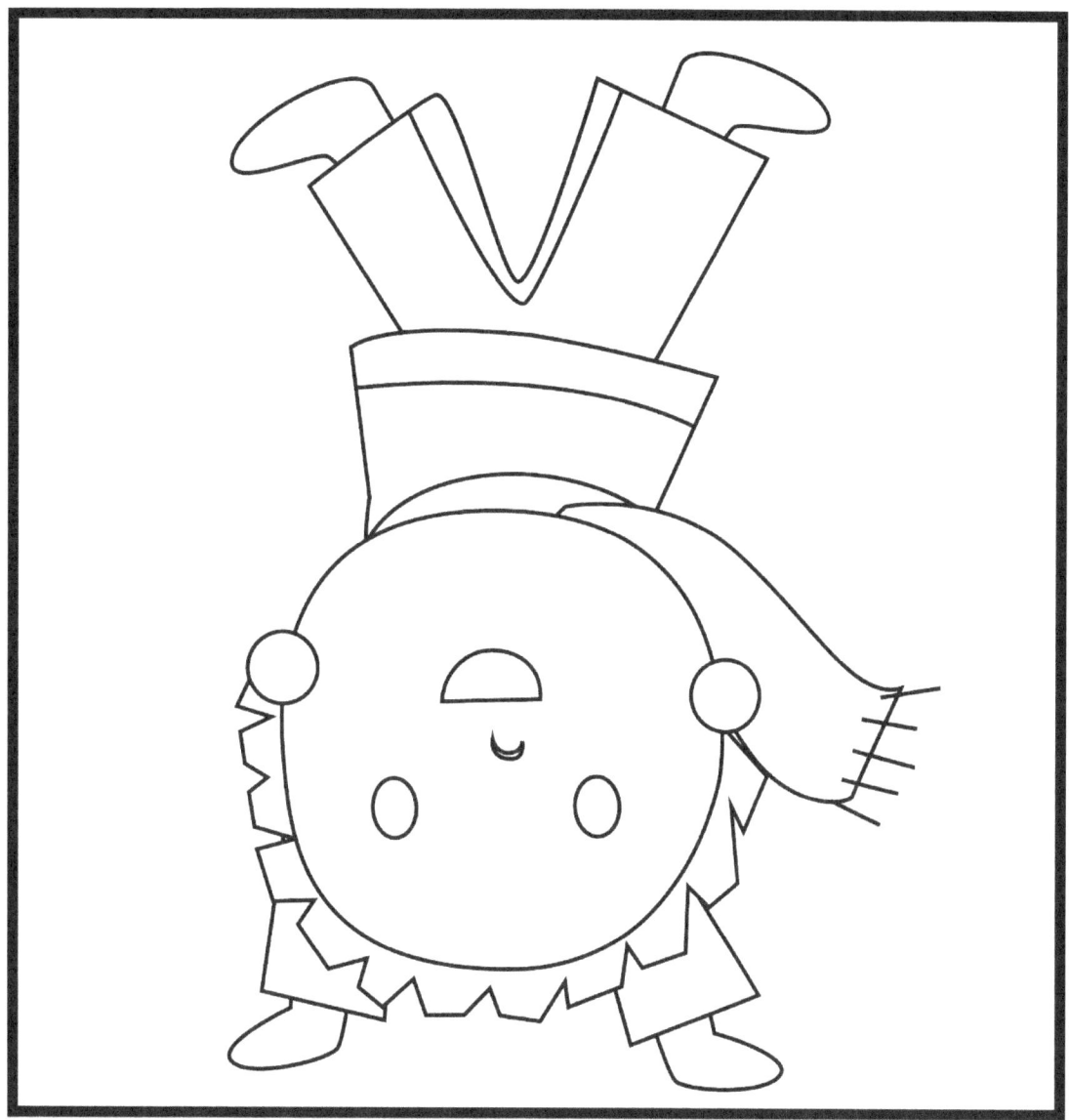

note:

_____

_____

_____

APRIL 47TH

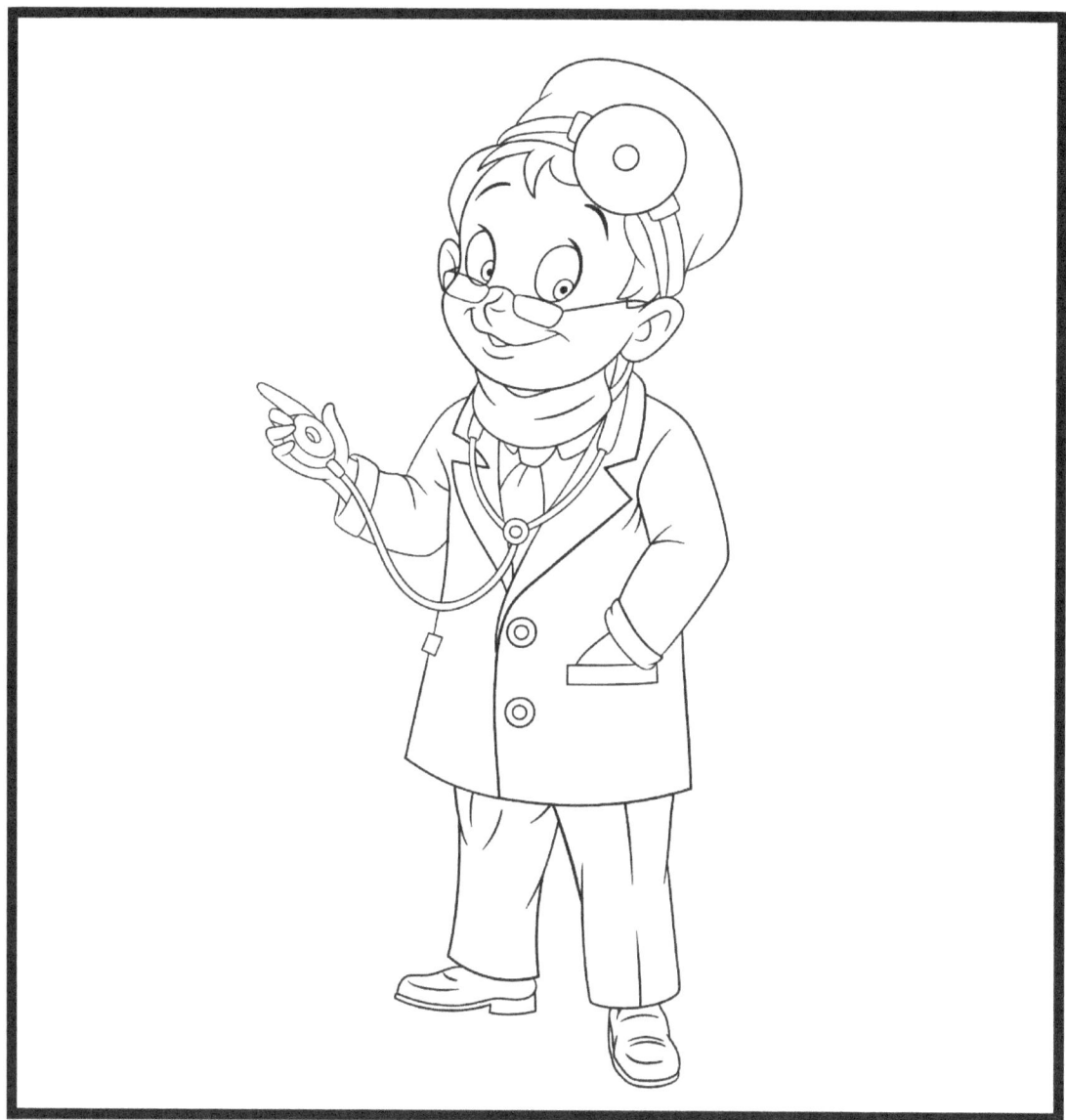

note:

_____

_____

_____

APRIL 48TH

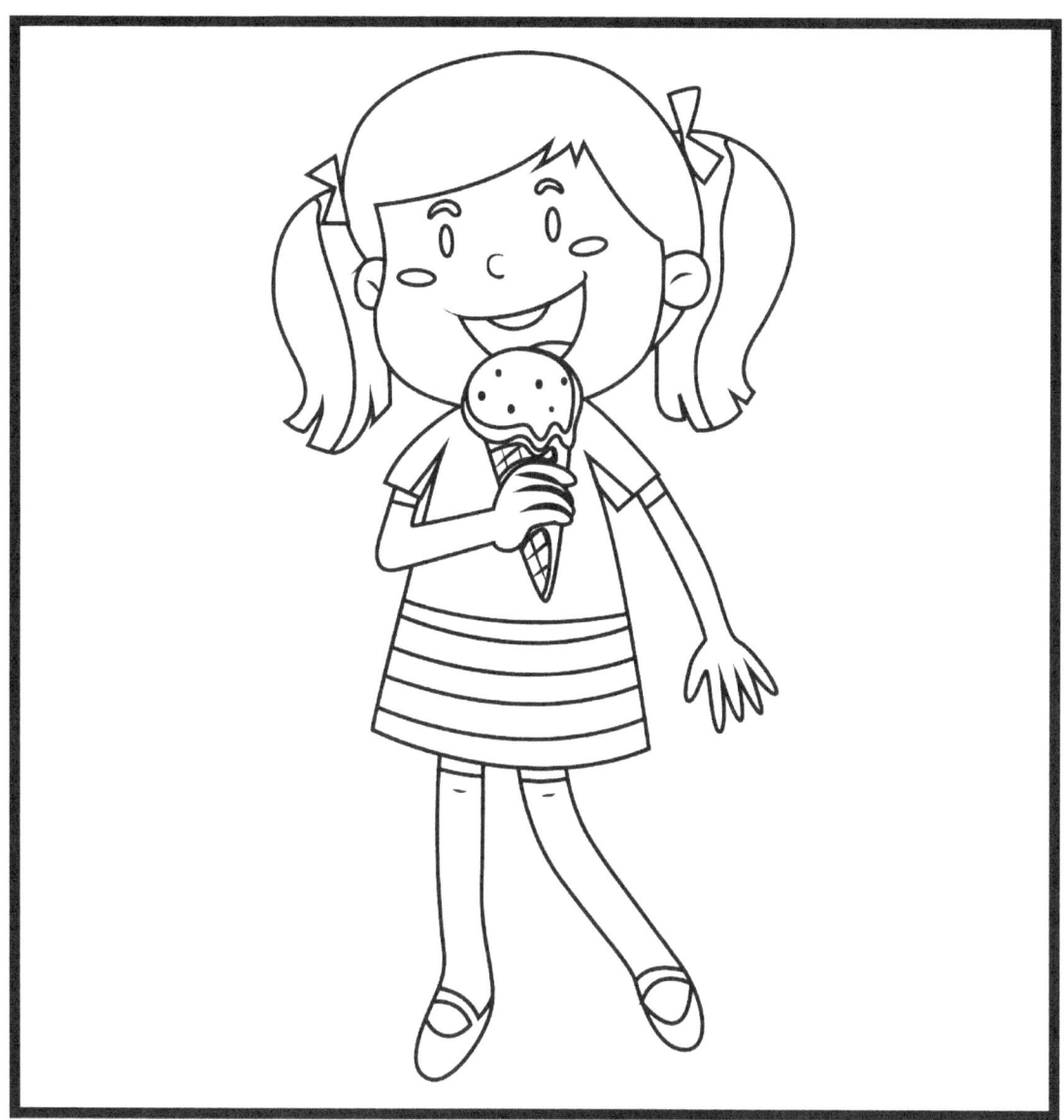

note:

_____

_____

_____

.

APRIL 49TH

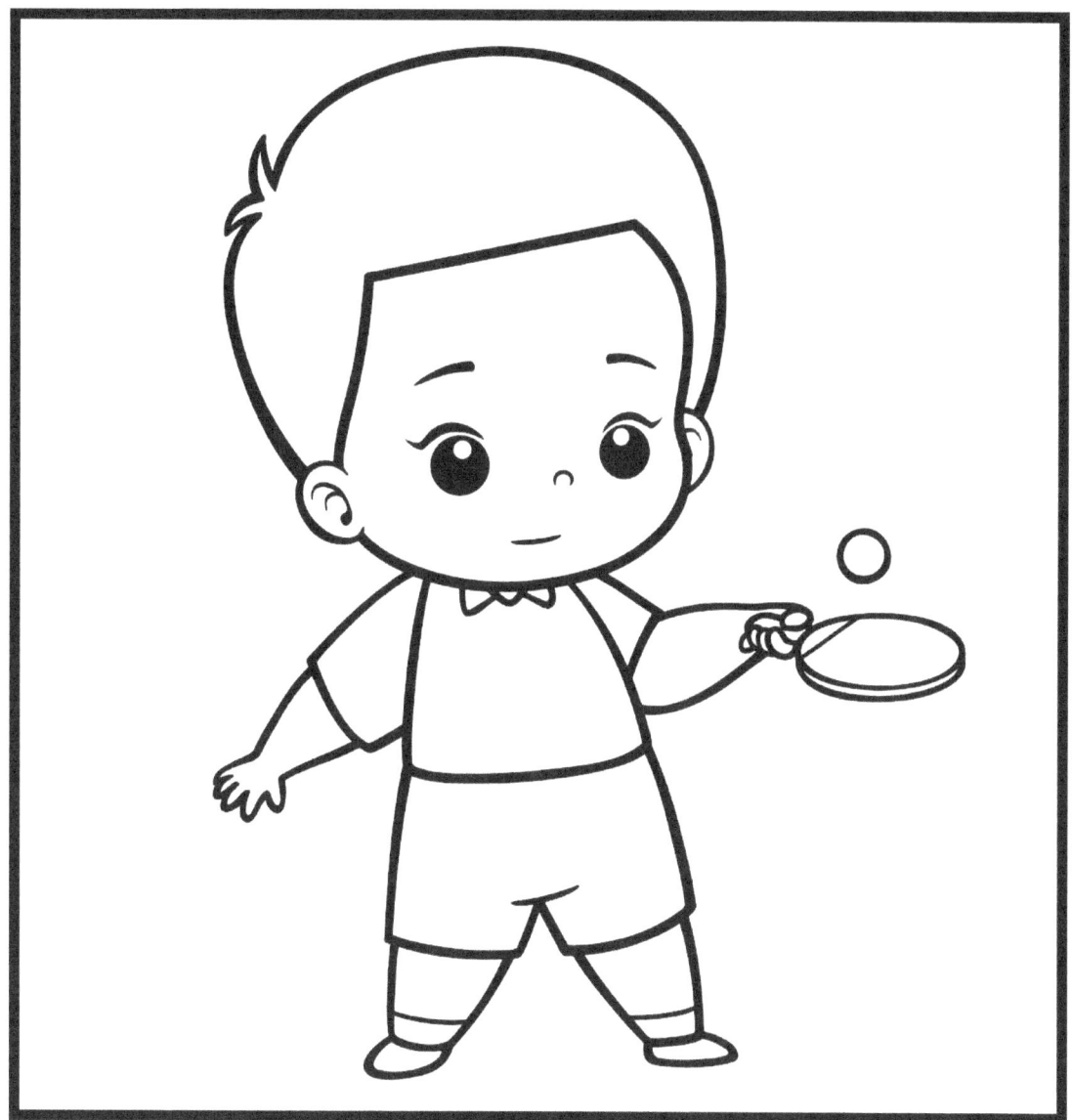

note:

_____

_____

_____

APRIL 50TH

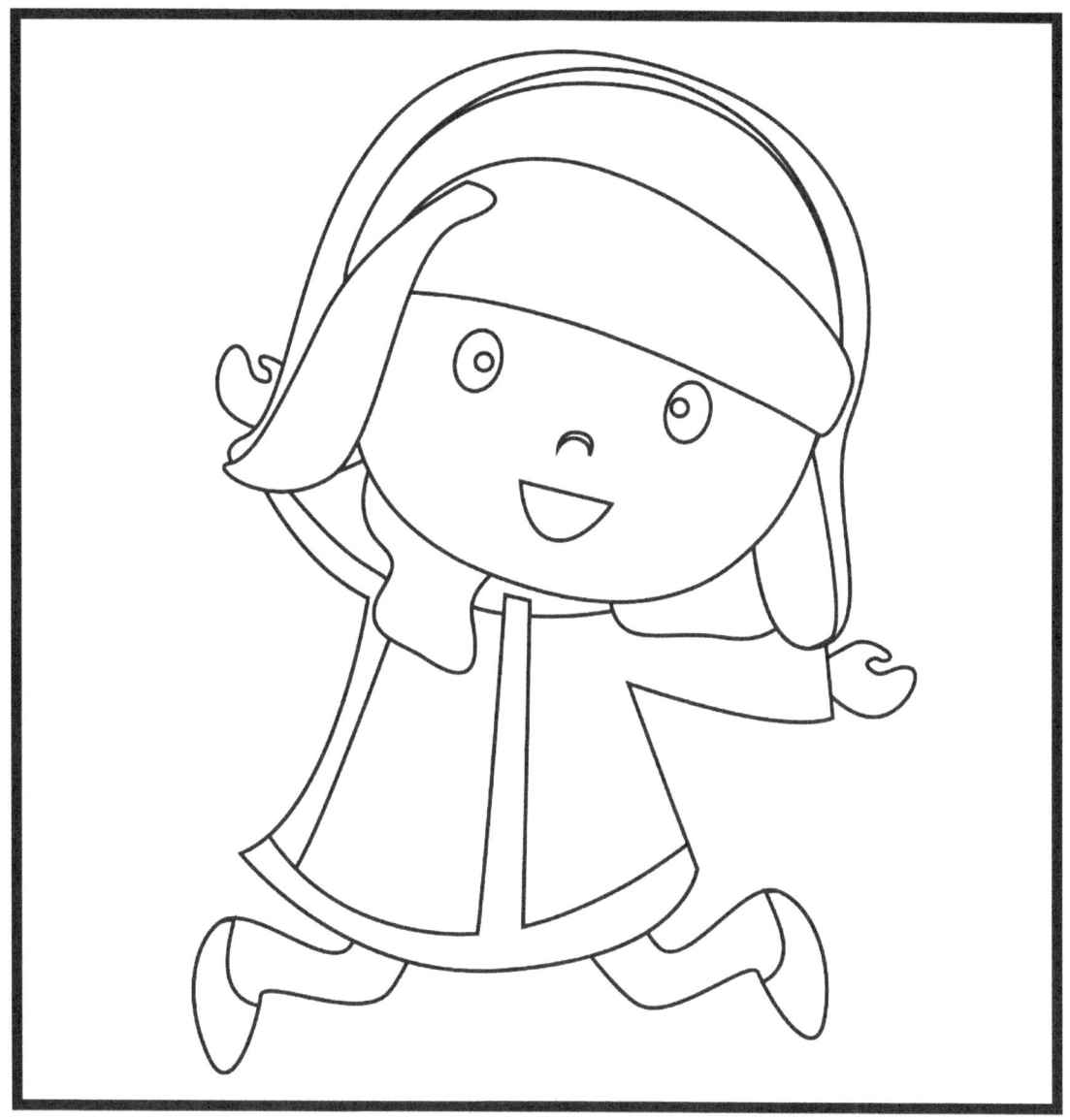

note:

_____

_____

_____